To: [handwritten]

Wake up, it's Gap-Time

Enjoy N.O.

&

Have fun reading the book

Martha Madden

Wake up, it's Gap-Time

A Guided Tour to Transitioning and Planning for Your Retirement Dreams

by Martha Ann Madden

Copyright © 2008 by Martha Ann Madden.

Library of Congress Control Number: 2008903340
ISBN: Hardcover   978-1-4363-3562-1
                 Softcover   978-1-4363-3561-4

All rights reserved. No part of this book may be reproduced or transmitted in any form or by any means, electronic or mechanical, including photocopying, recording, or by any information storage and retrieval system, without permission in writing from the copyright owner.

This book was printed in the United States of America.

To order additional copies of this book, contact:
Xlibris Corporation
1-888-795-4274
www.Xlibris.com
Orders@Xlibris.com
45781

CONTENTS

Introduction 13

Chapter 1 Aging is not optional, but growing old is 19

Chapter 2 Is your mind open? 28

Chapter 3 Awaken your creativity and
launch your future 41

Chapter 4 Stop playing it safe with employment and
life-long learning 54

Chapter 5 Relationships and finding social connections 67

Chapter 6 Healthy concerns 81

Chapter 7 Volunteer, be all you can be! 93

Chapter 8 All Gap-Timers want to do is
have some fun! 105

Chapter 9 One size does not fit all 116

Chapter 10 Are you stuck? 124

Chapter 11 Expect the unexpected 135

Chapter 12 Putting it all together 145

References 151

Martha's Bio 155

Dedication

Gap-Time is dedicated to all my family and friends who have given me support and encouragement over the years. Had it not been for them, I would not have been able to achieve the accomplishments which have brought me such enjoyment and pleasure in my life.

I am humbled and honored to consider these "special" friends as family. Realize that the words in this book come from our discussions and the advice they provided me. Now we will share with others.

In memory of Velma, James and Jimmy Madden.

Prayer for the Aged

Lord, thou knowest better than I know thyself that I am growing older.

Keep me from getting talkative, and particularly from the fatal habit of thinking I must say something on every occasion.

Release me from craving to try to straighten out everybody's affairs.

Keep my mind free from the recital of endless details—give me wings to get to the point.

I ask for grace enough to listen to the tales of others' pains. Help me to endure them with patience, but seal my lips on my aches and pains—they are increasing and my love of rehearsing them is there.

Keep me reasonably sweet; I do not want to be a saint—some of them are so hard to live with—but a sour old person is one of the crowning works of the devil.

Make me thoughtful, but not moody; helpful, but not bossy. With my vast store of wisdom, it seems a pity not to use it all—but thou knowest, Lord, that I want a few friends at the end.

—Found in the diary of my Mother, Velma Madden

Acknowledgements

I would like to especially thank Annette Sharp for her invaluable assistance in my own journey and the creation of this book, and Lori Welch for her great insight and creative input. A special thanks to all my *Gap-Time* friends who advised me and contributed their own insights, most notably Alta, Dianne, Gaynor, Jim, Dong, Deanne, Mark, Randy, Judy, Barney, Bess, Paul, Temple, Mary, Nick, and Ned.

Introduction

Retirement can represent a very meaningful, purposeful time in your life. Unfortunately, we've been programmed to think of retirement as little more than cross-country road trips, endless fishing excursions and lunches with friends. While that's great for the first two weeks, it will likely not nourish your soul for the long-term. The concept for this book was born out of my personal observations, research, and evaluation. As I began to think about slowing down and taking more time for leisure and learning activities, I discovered a lack of good information on this transition period, or *Gap-Time*, which is approximately six years before you retire and six years after that time. There is plenty of information available on financial planning. So what else do you need to plan for retirement besides finances? I knew what to do with my money, but what about information on stimulating the emotional, spiritual, and psychological part of life?

My major focus has always been on my professional and personal development. So now that it is time to slow down, many questions come to mind. What amount of time do I want to spend working, playing, volunteering, spending with family, friends, etc.? How "busy" do I want to be? What about where I live? Do I stay in my current location or look to move to a smaller city or a different state?

Surely you have questions beyond your retirement nest egg. What about relationships with your spouse or significant other, your adult children or your grandchildren, other family members and/or friends? Do you currently have a meaningful relationship with all of them? How will more time on your hands impact those relationships? Do you want a closeness that you don't presently enjoy? What if there is no family? What about your leisure interests? Are there certain activities that you currently participate in that you wish to continue? Has your career been keeping you from activities you now have time to explore? What about your health? Do you maintain an exercise and eating regime that promotes optimal health? Will you focus on optimal health once you retire? Are you going to return to work? Will you change job focus or continue doing something that is similar to your existing job? Is spirituality important in your life now? Will spirituality be important when you retire? How will you handle time alone? Can you handle change? How adaptable are you to new situations, places, people, and experiences? Do you plan on living in the same house or will you move to another house? Do you plan to continue living where you are now or do you plan to relocate to another city, state, or country?

Reading usually provides me with abundant suggestions on my topics of interest, but there is a clear "gap" of information on this period of time I have identified as the *Gap-Time*. The more I talked with business associates, family, and friends about their retirement plans, the more I understood the need for *Gap-Time*. Planning your financial goals is important, but there are many, many other areas that require planning and consideration as well. As an educator and consultant, I have lived my life experiencing and sharing those experiences with others in the areas of business development, educational opportunities, environmental management, networking, and problem solving. I am delighted to share my *Gap-Time* knowledge, resources, discoveries and insights with you. I've brought some of my friends along on the journey as well—I'll introduce them at various points throughout the upcoming Chapters.

Gap-Time is designed to be a resource for you as you begin to think about your options, and a reference for you to return to as your journey unfolds. My hope is that I save you some steps and head-scratching sessions with what I've learned through research, experimentation and many, many conversations—many with myself!

The first stage of *Gap-Time* is "this time" in your life when you are thinking about retiring or will retire. The pressure of current business, putting out client fires, getting more work and/or clients clouds our ability to satisfy our intellectual curiosity so that by the time we are considering retirement, we need to re-introduce our "self" to our "self." I've included some great exercises to help you in this self-discovery phase. *Gap-Time* allows you to take a step back and observe your home and work environments and identify the system of interacting variables that brings you success and happiness. It is about rising above the ordinary and clearly understanding the significant opportunities and possibilities before and during retirement.

The second stage is the six years after you've left your "position." Because *Gap-Time* is about you and discovering the unique way you want to retire, it is a continuous journey and not a static plan. You will want to revisit your *Gap-Time* plan several times during your journey and make appropriate adjustments.

Each of us has a different vision of the period after they leave their day job. It is certainly different from our parents' retirement, when one received a gold watch on his/her way out the door and went home to sit in the rocking chair. Personally speaking, I have never had any interest in totally checking out of the professional world, but surely some of you can't wait to trade your suits and laptops in for waders and a tackle box never looking back. "I have no intention of retiring," says our friend Gerlinde. "I work and that is my entertainment, and it provides me with socialization." Well, Gerlinde, I'm here to tell you that you can bring those same things to your *Gap-Time* life. Mary, a part-time CPA, thinks along the same lines as Gerlinde. Retirement for her means to "lay down and die . . . My aunt told me that old accountants never die, they just lose their balance." Mary enjoys being semi-retired, but wishes that she had planned for more activity which would have provided her with more structure. We hear and see all the messages about financial planning when it comes to retirement, but there aren't any messages telling us to plan for our "self" and what we'll do to live meaningful lives once we've left our "day jobs." There are others, however, like our friend Father Jim, who embraces retirement for the options and choices it represents. Retirement is when you get to "do all the things you didn't have time to do before. To retire means I do what I want to do when I want to do it," says Father Jim. Although he believes that priests don't retire, they just fade away, he does suggest planning for an inspiring life. It is my wish for all our *Gap-Timers* to P-L-A-N for and live an inspired, inspiring life and to be open and optimistic to what lies ahead.

    If you're reading this book, you probably know that you want to "slow down" one day, but you are not sure what you should be doing at what time. There are tens of thousands of financial agencies available to guide your financial planning for retirement and almost as many to help you plan leisure activities. You will find few agencies and professionals, however, to help you in preparation for, and during, retirement for the emotional, physical, psychological, and spiritual sides. If your wish is to do more than take back-to-back cruises or hang out at Disney World with the grandkids, you're in the right place. *Gap-Time* is NOT financial planning; it is "you" planning.

Gap-Time directs your conceptualizing, visioning, and understanding of yourself to promote the shape of your future. I hope you find enjoyment in defining and re-defining your purpose and vision as you build a creative retirement plan. It is my wish that whatever you create for yourself, your plan bridges the "*Gap-Time.*"

Gap-Time is one of adventure, excitement, and wonderment. If you are ready to explore new ways of living in retirement (slowing down) through inspiration and defining your life's meaning and purpose, let's get started.

~~~Martha A. Madden

The only joy in the world is to begin.

Cesare Pave (The Little Zen Companion)

Chapter 1

Aging is not optional, but growing old is

"The tragedy of old age is not that one is old, but that one is young."
—Oscar Wilde, *The Picture of Dorian Gray*.

Researching the topic of retirement was an experience by itself. Approximately 85 % of the literature focuses attention on financial planning for retirement. While financial planning is a very important aspect of a successful retirement, as previously mentioned, it is not the only one. *Gap-Time* focuses on the emotional, psychological, and philosophical information on the non-financial side of retirement. During a 30- to 40-year work span, you will spend an average of 62,400 to 83,200 actual work hours attached to a life style of routine, training, institutional knowledge, product awareness, client satisfaction, and more. "The average American spends more than 90,000 hours working towards retirement but fewer than 10 hours actually planning for it" (Cullinane, J & Fitzgerald, C., 2007). In the U.S. alone, more than 10,000 people retire every day! (Johnson, R., 2001).

Art Linkletter joined Mark Victor Hansen in writing a book, *How to Make the Rest of Your Life the Best of Your Life* (Hansen, M. V. & Linkletter, A., 2006). Perhaps you are young enough to remember Mr. Linkletter's television and radio shows. In a recent interview with Mr. Linkletter about his 28th book, Art provided his philosophy of life as "throwing himself into a variety of causes and businesses that he's passionate about: from research on Alzheimer's disease to promoting alternative energy sources" (Crane, 2007). Mr. Linkletter turned 95 in July 2007. In response to a question by the interviewer on what drives him to stay so busy at his age, Mr. Linkletter's response was, "I like to be around people who talk and write and never stop. I came up the hard way—I was a poor kid and I always worked and have enjoyed it ever since. I haven't needed to work for awhile but I still do. I've written 28 books, three of them autobiographies. In my life, I've met a lot of interesting people. Talking to people, writing books and raising money keep me interested in a lot of different ways in life. I've never retired—I spent the first third of my life as a poor kid, the second third as a radio, TV and movie star and in business. In this last third of my life I am giving back through volunteering—it's very rewarding" (Crane, 2007).

Clearly, Mr. Linkletter had a vision. If the vision wasn't what he wanted to do, I bet he knew that he didn't want to—sit at home in a rocking chair. By the way, volunteering is a great way to add meaning and inspiration to your *Gap-Time*, and I've dedicated an entire chapter on the subject.

"There is no way we can look forward to our aging if we see the journey that is life as moving upward to a peak in our 40s and then abruptly dropping off into a period of physical decline in which we remain suspended for 40 or 50 years until our eventual death" (Harkness, H., 1999). So what age is "old" nowadays, and what age is retirement age? I remember when I received my first piece of mail from AARP. It was that stark realization—that J-O-L-T—that maybe, just maybe I was entering into the zone of "old" age. It meant that I had to start making decisions and reviewing how I was living, as well as where. It was time to start thinking about change, which doesn't have to be a bad and/or negative thing. Age is just a number. I'm a firm believer that you can be youthful at any age; just ask one of my dearest friends, Dianne. Turning 65 meant two things to her. "I was able to save lots of money by going on Medicare, and I became a card carrying member of 'old.' I wanted to be old and foxy, however, so I went out and bought myself a new Jaguar," laughs Dianne. "It's midnight blue and beautiful," Dianne continues in her delightfully charming Southern accent. "My son says it's like putting a plow on a race horse. Apparently, he thinks I drive it too slow, but I don't care. I just glide and wave." I'm going to be sharing more about Dianne later because she is an awesome testament to finding creative ways to not only enjoy, but really blossom in your *Gap-Time*.

"'Old' is still 15 years off into the future" (Henderson, N., 2007, September 12). That's 15 years from whatever age you are now. Most folks in their 50s are just starting to think about retirement with the understanding that they are not quite ready to retire. In effect, they are putting "old" on hold. So is the new "40" really age 60? Many of us have been putting old on hold for years. For a while, I was holding off old by pulling out gray hairs as soon as they arrived. I've now enlisted the help of my stylist, Ned, in my quest to make age just a number. I'm sure if you asked any stylist in your hometown, he/she would be able to provide you with a pretty big list of those who share the same quest. We're fighting the battle to look young because we feel young. Thanks to improved lifestyles, advancements in medicine, and many other things we've been blessed with in our lifetime, we are younger than our parents were at our age. More and more people are enjoying a more youthful "old" age, hence the need for *Gap-Time*. *Gap-Timers* aren't thinking about retirement homes, they're thinking about second homes and second careers. They're planning for the next chapter in their life, not their funeral.

Why do we retire at the age we do? Germany is often credited with originating the retirement age. However, a number of policy-level decisions in the United States staked a claim of "65" as the magic number for more conclusive reasons. Germany adopted a social insurance program in 1889 that provided support for those who were disabled from work by age. Germany initially set the retirement age at 70, and it wasn't until 1916 that the age was lowered to 65. The Committee on Economic Security (CES) first proposed retirement at age 65 under Social Security in 1935. The decision was based on prevailing retirement ages in private pension systems in existence at the time and the 30 state "old-age" pension systems in operation. Half of those pension systems used age 65 as the retirement age and half used age 70. In 1934, Congress passed the federal Railroad Retirement System that used age 65 as its retirement age. Age 65 was determined a more reasonable retirement age than age 70 by the CES. Actuarial studies confirmed this choice. Using age 65 produced a manageable system that would be made self-sustaining with modest levels of payroll taxation. We won't debate the worthiness of that statement in this book. With life expectancy increasing by 10, 20, or even 30 years from that in 1934, understanding not only the impacts of persons age 65 and older on society, but the opportunities that this group of individuals is seeking—and what opportunities are available—in the next 10 to 20 years is the focus of this book. Starting in 2011, when the first baby boomers turn

65, experts project a major wave of retirement (Waxman, B. & Mendelson, R. A., 2006). By 2050, there will be more than 86.7 million people over the age of 65 in the United States (Waxman, B. & Mendelson, R. A., 2006).

"With the first wave of the 80 million baby boomers headed toward retirement, Washington, D.C.'s suburbs are planning for what Virginia's Fairfax County Supervisor T. Dana Kauffman calls the 'silver tsunami'—when the percentage of those 65 and older in many suburban counties is expected to double over the next 20 years. The population shift mirrors what is happening nationally and will be so significant, lawmakers and experts say, that it will affect every aspect of municipal government, including transportation, health services and public safety" (Gowen, A., 2007, September 16). What we'll be seeing is a shift from our parents' view of retirement—rocking chairs and afternoons at the playground with the grandkids—to a new, more meaningful/purposeful part of the journey. The "old" retirement mirrors thoughts of isolation; loss of purpose; termination/ending; routine and monotony; dependency and passivity; declining health and vitality.

Gap-Timers are pursuing the "new" retirement, which uses terms such as transformation and positive change; creative purpose; life balance and personal fulfillment; exploration and discovery; involvement; renewal; passion and new beginnings. *Gap-Time* doesn't represent an ending; it represents a beginning. It represents a shift or a positive change which is yours to embrace (Johnson, R.P, 2001). It is the gift of time at a stage in your life when you have the experience and maturity to recognize it for what it represents. It is yours to do with as you desire—with a strong emphasis on the word "desire." You can use it to pursue your dormant dreams, re-discover a passionate pastime, or explore a new interest. My friend Dong is a boomer who isn't at the age for retirement as of this writing, but I wanted to get his thoughts on the subject for this book. He's enjoyed a great career in the federal government as a chemical/environmental engineer for over 20 years.

"Certainly the next phase of life after government service has steadily moved forward from the back of my mind. I blame the media, the commercials on TV. The airway messages that provide the flood of panic about my part of the baby-boom generation who should have planned for retirement." Dong, however, has not let the media hype overtake his personal message about retirement. To Dong, retirement represents another phase of his life. He is looking at it as a "timed," or "scheduled" promotion. Well said, Dong. *Gap-Time* is a step up, and you get to decide what your promotion is going to be. "When I think of retiring, I think of retooling for another phase of life," says Dong. "Slowing down is not what I think of, but rather rebalancing and refocusing for a promotion."

Aging is like death and taxes. We can't stop it, so we might as well embrace it. In my younger days, I used to snow ski and play a lot of tennis. It was something I greatly enjoyed. I found it to be a great stress reliever, as well as an excellent way to stay physically, as well as mentally, fit. I enjoyed the occasional game of golf as well, although I was never much of a player. When asked what my handicap was, my reply was always, "serious." As I began to age, my abilities at both of my favored pastimes began to decline. It was tough to accept both mentally and emotionally, but I never let what I couldn't do be my focus. I shifted my thinking and focused on new things to try. Some people are never good at tennis or golf so I felt fortunate that I was able to enjoy both for as long as I did. Eventually, I hung up my racket and clubs, and exchanged them for a gym membership and a pair of walking shoes. I also enjoy dancing as a form of exercise. I don't feel like I gave anything up in the name of old age; I shifted my thinking and re-aligned my activities. As a result, I've met some fabulous new friends at the gym and at various dances I've attended. My world hasn't shrunk as a result—it's broadened! One of my best friends, Temple, likes to remind me that my voice hasn't weakened. What do you think she means by that?

The current trend is that older adults are healthier, better educated, and more active than ever—negating the myth that a lifestyle of leisure is the only correct way to retire. There are numerous aging myths that have been debunked in recent years. *Gap-Timers* are enjoying more fulfilling lives in their 50s, 60s, 70s, 80s, and beyond. Art Linkletter and millions of others live with the understanding that aging is not optional, but growing old is. Regardless of how good your stylist is and/or how many medical advancements are made, the key to enjoying your life is your attitude. Attitude is everything. *Gap-Time* helps you explore the possibilities and plan for the non-financial side of retirement in an organized, creative and fun way, but you must bring a positive attitude.

As you read through the Chapters, I ask you to make the following shifts in your thoughts and words with regard to your *Gap-Time*.

Shift From Thoughts of:

Loss of Purpose/Job
Isolation
Immobility
Hibernation
Depression
Reclusiveness
Washed Up
Over-the-Hill
Idleness

Elderly
Routine
Monotony
Dependency
Passivity
Apathy
Resignation
Frustration
Boredom
Declining Health
"Out to Pasture"

Shift to Thoughts of . . .

Transformation
Positive Change
Personal Evaluation and Assessment
Creative Expression
Life Purpose
Self-Empowerment
Personal Fulfillment
Life Balance
Exploration and Discovery
Life-Long Learning
Renewal
Personal Accomplishment
Social Interaction
Passion
Social Connectivity
Involvement
Participation
Activity

Personal Growth
New Beginnings!
Gap-Timers with a positive attitude and a sense of adventure may now proceed.

Ah but I was so much older then; I'm younger than that now.

Bob Dylan (The Little Zen Companion)

Chapter 2

Is your mind open?

"What lies behind us and what lies before us are tiny matters compared to what lies within us."
—Ralph Waldo Emerson

Is your mind open so you can open your life? The first step of our *Gap-Time* journey is to gather information on ourselves in order to open windows in your life that you may have previously closed and/or thought were closed. According to Tao Te Ching, "He who knows others is wise. He who knows himself is enlightened." In order to discover your possibilities, you must first start with some self-discovery. Annually, hundreds of thousands of individuals attempt to transition into something "different" without investing any, or very little, time into researching and understanding the possibilities for retirement, let alone taking the time to research and understand their own "self." The crush of daily living keeps many of us from knowing our true self and from consciously moving beyond routine to creative. We know that we are special, we have purpose, but we cannot identify the last time we took the opportunity to honor that part of us. If you need a little reminder, pull out awards you've received in the past, and pat yourself on the back. Perhaps you've received glowing letters of recommendation from past employers or clients. Give them a quick read. It doesn't matter if the letter was from your Mom—if it makes you feel good, drag it out.

Remember and be proud of all of those great achievements you accomplished. (More importantly—know that many more achievements lie ahead!) Be good to yourself. When I need a little reminder, I pull out letters from my students thanking me for scholarships they received through my family. Many of them include a special experience we shared, and it transports me to a different time in my life. All of them, however, remind me of my accomplishments and how, sometimes unknowingly, I've touched peoples' lives. It reminds me that my life has a purpose, and that I am a unique, special person. As you recall your past, realize that there are many, many more achievements to be made. As an example, in the midst of writing this book, I received an honorary Doctorate of Humane Letters conferred on me by Dr. Webb, president of Northwestern State University. There is still plenty more expected of you in your *Gap-Time*.

Some of you may be feeling uncomfortable or even guilty for taking the time to focus on yourself. Take care of yourself first. "Selfishness has gotten a bad reputation . . . . If you can't take care of yourself, you're going to be dependent and needy . . . . One of my favorite philosophers, the King—Elvis Presley, of course—had TCB (takin' care of business) as his motto. If you're taking care of business and *you're* the business at hand, it makes no sense to feel guilty, you're just doing your job" (Browne, J., 1998). Focusing on yourself is not something to feel guilty about—it's your job to be the CEO of you. If you're not happy, it's pretty doubtful that those people sitting around you are going to be happy either. You're the expert on you. You're the only person who really knows whether or not going back to work part-time is going to make you happy. You may be the only one who knows that you hate the thought of retiring to Florida. Speak up; now's your chance.

As you proceed through the chapters to follow (and through your *Gap-Time* for that matter), give yourself permission to be a "beginner" in the development of your *Gap-Time* plan. Transitioning to retirement means reconnecting to yourself. In gathering information about who you are, we will start by identifying your most significant values. Your personal values are those you take for yourself and that are apparent in your attitudes, beliefs, and actions. Circle the values below that best characterize you and feel free to add some of your own.

Accomplishment accountability accuracy adventure all for one and one for all beauty calm peace challenge change cleanliness orderliness collaboration commitment communication community competence competition concern for others continuous improvement cooperation love of country creativity customer satisfaction decisiveness dedicated democracy discipline direction discovery efficiency equality excellence fairness faith family freedom friendship good will gratitude hard working harmony honesty independence inner peace innovation integrity justice knowledge leadership love loyalty meaning merit money openness peace perfection perseverance personal growth pleasure positive attitude power practicality preservation privacy problem solving prosperity punctuality quality of work regulation and control resourcefulness respect for others results-oriented safety satisfying others security self-givingness self-reliance service simplicity skill spirit in life status strength a will to succeed success teamwork timeliness tolerance tradition tranquility trust truth wealth women's rights unity variety wisdom

In the box below, write in the 10 most significant values that best describe you on a daily basis.

On a daily basis, I operate with the following 10 values:

Next, let's explore people, places, and things that are most important in your life. Phillip C. McGraw (Dr. Phil) asks his readers to identify what is important to them as individuals. "I want you to start asking yourself what is important to you: What do you want? What do you need to be part of your life?" (McGraw, P. C., 2001). Drawing from some of the examples provided by Dr. Phil, let's examine what is important in our life now and in the immediate future.

In the following exercise, we'll see what is important to you now and what you think will be important to you in the future (next five to 10 years). These are things that your life would feel incomplete without. Feel free to add more of your own in the lines provided. Using Columns 2 & 3 (how you feel about them now [Column 2] and how you think you'll feel about them in the future [Column 3]), please rank each item according to the following:

1—Not Important
2—Somewhat Important
3—Very Important

Areas of Importance in My Life	How Important Are They in My Life **Now?**	How Important Will They Be in My Life in the **Future?** (five to 10 years)
Music		
Art		
Work		
Kids		
Grandchildren		
Spiritual Life		
Free Time		
Pride in Work		
Pride in Appearance		
Living with Dignity		
Health		
A Career that uses my strengths		
Volunteer Work		
Hobbies		
Physical Activity		
Independence		

Meaningful Relationship		
Different Body Type		
Feeling Like a Giver		
Educational Endeavors		
Travel Opportunities		
_____		
_____		

Select two of your top rankings from your future column (Column 3) and write them in the left column below. Write down how you would meet that need in the column to the right of that one. Read your results to two other people and write down their suggestions for an action plan for those areas in the designated columns. It helps if they have that same area of importance in their lives.

Here's an example.

Areas of Importance that I plan to keep or to attain five to 10 years from now	My Action Plan to Keep or Maintain that Area of Importance in My Life	Person #1's Recommended Action Plan to Keep or Maintain that Area of Importance in One's Life	Person #2's Recommended Action Plan to Keep or Maintain that Area of Importance in One's Life
Spiritual Life	Attend Sunday Worship.	Attend churches, synagogues, mosques, temples, places of	Rethink the religious practices and beliefs from your childhood and consider whether

			worship and meditation that you never have.	they still make sense.
Physical Activity	Walk three miles, three days a week.	Try skiing, snowboarding, jet skiing, hang gliding, parasailing, surfing, and anything that pushes the limits of your comfort zone.	Perform your routine differently such as walking backwards, or walking with your eyes closed.
Travel Opportunities	Travel three times a year within the U.S. with family.	Travel by yourself.	Travel using an "outsider's" view such as using only a bike or only your two feet or only public transportation.

Now it's your turn.

Areas of Importance that I plan to keep or to attain five to 10 years from now	My Action Plan to Keep or Maintain that Area of Importance in My Life	Person #1's Recommended Action Plan to Keep or Maintain that Area of Importance in One's Life	Person #2's Recommended Action Plan to Keep or Maintain that Area of Importance in One's Life

If you need different ways to think about the "routine," there's a unique website called *wikiHow (The How-to Manual That You Can Edit)*. There are many entertaining and thought-provoking "how to" topics, including an exercise to open your mind (*http://www.wikihow.com/Exercise-an-Open-Mind*, 2007). The recommendations compel the reader to make changes in the routine. Many of the recommendations suggest doing something different from your current way of doing things, such as taking unusual classes; taking up physical activities that you have not tried before; working crossword puzzles every day; joining clubs based on things you have no knowledge of; and many more creative activities.

In the box below, list how you would spend your free time if you never had to work another day in your life. If you're feeling artistic, by all means sketch out your vision.

If I never had to work another day, I would . . .

In the next box, pretend your life is ending and list what you would regret not doing, seeing, or achieving?

I regret not ever . . .

The *Gap-Time* journey directs your attention to the task of memorializing the essence of you. Circle the adjectives below that you think describe the full potential of you, now and in the future (McGraw, P. C., 2001).

pretty attractive beautiful cute nice-looking appealing cool sweet spiritual wise nice friendly faithful leader strong supportive moral ethical principled good honest decent warm loving tender warmhearted demonstrable caring kind affectionate cordial hospitable welcoming amiable cheerful passionate fiery enthusiastic zealous arrogant egocentric altruistic sympathetic humane selfless philanthropic smart dependent free gentle thoughtful domineering submissive autonomous creative compassionate self-sufficient private liberated conventional objective elegant clever stylish intelligent quick charming tidy neat thoughtful attentive careful watchful alert reliable inspired inventive resourceful ingenious productive exciting energetic lively vigorous bouncy active joyful blissful pleased ecstatic cheery sane rational sensible reasonable normal complete capable genuine inspiring proud approachable peaceful honest giving nurturing accomplished whole perfect undivided achiever great confident at ease relaxed able knowledgeable skilled proficient expert adept rich wealthy affluent prosperous full gorgeous valuable abundant

Have a family member or a friend that you trust review your adjectives and listen to their comments. Were they generally supportive of your choices? Did they add superlatives? Did they disagree with your choices? This is a reality check for you.

In the next two boxes, list what strengths and weaknesses other people have commented on about you and then list what strengths and weaknesses you see in yourself.

Strengths Others See In You:

Strengths You See in Yourself:

Weaknesses Others See in You:

Weaknesses You See in Yourself:

Now describe your "best" self in the box below.

The best me is:

So far we have identified your key values—what is important in your life (today and in the future), your strengths and weaknesses, and the "best" you. Using that information, you will now create your personal mission statement. Write it in the first person and make statements about the future you hope to achieve. Start with the two "Areas of Importance" you completed earlier. Write the statements as if you are already making them happen, such as "I am so happy and grateful now that I _____ ." (fill in the blank).

Here's one example of a personal vision statement.

> I am so happy and grateful now that I: read and write every day; publish books; share a lifetime of knowledge about people, management, and workplaces with a vast international audience; positively impact every person with whom I come in contact; live a life dedicated to integrity, commitment, challenge, and joy; share my deepest love with my husband and value my marriage; spend time valuing a few close friends; spend time valuing family relationships; invent and write about recipes and food; travel the world to experience its richness; watch plays and movies; listen to music; never have to worry about spending money on anything I want; etc.

Now write your personal vision statement.

> I am . . .

In the next box, list the differences between your personal vision statement and how you are currently living.

> The differences between my vision statement and how I am currently living are:

In the next box, list the possible challenges or obstacles to attaining your vision.

> Challenges or obstacles to attaining my vision could be:

In the next box, list the people, places and activities that allow you to most fully feel your "natural" self.

> I am my most natural self when . . .

    Jack Canfield, co-creator of the *Chicken Soup for the Soul* series, talks about how to get from where you are to where you want to be in his book, *The Success Principles*. "To face what's not working in your life usually means you're going to have to do something uncomfortable. It means you might have to exercise more self-discipline, confront somebody, risk not being liked, ask for what you want, demand respect instead of settling for an abusive relationship, or maybe even quit your job" (Canfield, J., 2005). In other words, you must take responsibility for your life, your own happiness, and your own *Gap-Time*.

    Armed with information about "you," we are onto the next step of our *Gap-Time* journey. Are you ready?

Search back into your own vision—think back to the mind that thinks. Who is it?

Wu-Men (The Little Zen Companion)

Chapter 3

Awaken your creativity and launch your future

"Go confidently in the direction of your dreams! Live the life you've imagined."

—Henry David Thoreau

Create the details of your *Gap-Time* plan to fit your own needs. The emphasis is on the word, "create." For some of us, our creativity has burned out by the time we get to retire. Some of that void of creativity is due in large part to burnout. You have given too much of yourself to other people, or become so involved in your clients and keeping them happy, or measuring your success by the number of clients you have or the income you generate, that you have forgotten about you. Burnout robs us of a rich existence. Right after I left my role as Dean of Women/Student Life in the South at Northeast Louisiana University, I experienced serious burnout. I would be seated at home trying to *relax*. The phone would ring, and I would jump three feet out of my chair thinking that I needed to respond to some emergency or problem at a dorm. Maybe a student was hurt. Maybe there was a fire. Maybe a water main had burst. My brain had grown so accustomed to putting out fires that my body didn't know how to act once the fires were gone from my life. It took quite awhile after that time to settle back into another routine at another job. The key is to be alert to your responses and reactions to what is going on in your daily life. As you know, stress over the long term is not good so develop your own coping techniques if you haven't already. Taking long walks always helps me.

Perhaps you remember the book by Robert Fulghum, *All I Really Need To Know I Learned in Kindergarten*. Fulghum draws attention to lessons that are taught in kindergarten that if practiced today, would keep all of us grounded and balanced. One of those lessons is stated, "Live a balanced life—learn some and think some and draw and paint and sing and dance and play and work every day some" (Fulghum, R., 1986). So where do we go, or what do we do to recapture what we learned in kindergarten? To tap into that knowledge, you need to put on your play clothes. Seriously. Remember that positive attitude we mentioned earlier? In order to resurrect your creativity (yes—we all have some), you need to adopt a playful attitude. Close your eyes and envision something fun you used to do—not for work or for family—something you did just for you. Maybe you were 12 years old the last time you did it. Maybe it involved a coloring book or finger paints. It doesn't matter. Maybe you were at the ocean with your watercolors. Chances are you're stuck and are having a hard time recalling anything fun. That's normal for burnout folks. This may take awhile, but keep those eyes closed and something will pop across your mental screen. Did you used to collect stamps? Play tennis? Draw cartoons? Make and bake cookies?

Daniel Pink asserts in his book, *A Whole New Mind*, that creativity is becoming increasingly important (Pink, D., 2005). "A friend asked me what I would do with 547,600 if I were given it as a gift. I immediately rattled off a list of things I would buy. Then he told me he was not referring to money; he meant the number of minutes in a year—far more precious commodities than dollars. We are careful about how we budget our finances, but give far less thought to how we spend our time—or even more importantly, how we spend our spirit during those minutes. Every moment is an opportunity to feed your soul. The quality of your life depends on how much you are willing to let life love you" (Cohen, A. H., 2002). Every day presents an opportunity to say "yes" to life.

A study of engineers working for a major oil company was commissioned to examine what management considered was a lack of creativity. After months of asking questions ranging from where they grew up to what their educational backgrounds were to what their favorite colors were, the conclusions drawn were that creative people thought they were creative, and the less creative people didn't think they were (von Oech, 1998). So before we go on, check the box next to the response that best represents you.

I am creative.

YES ☐ NO ☐

Dr. Wayne Dyer calls creativity, inspiration—being connected to Source, being in-Spirit. "We know that there's something deep within us waiting to be known, which we sometimes call a 'gut reaction' to life's events. We have a built-in yearning to seek our inspired self and feel wholeness, a kind of inexplicable sense that patiently demands recognition and action" (Dyer, W. W., 2006). Creativity can also be formed through connectivity or being in a state of connectedness. First, you have to look beyond how you perceive yourself and the world. Then become aware of your life and how you interact with the world (Dreamer, O. M., 2005).

Creativity is certainly "channeled" by other factors that are uniquely "you." You are a far more complex organism today than the person you were at birth. You are a compilation of heredity, environment, education, and so much more. Your creativity was largely a function of your heredity, your environment, and your education. Creativity moves along the lines of the various intelligences. Enrichment of creativity will generally follow those intelligences.

One of my fondest memories comes from a time very early in my life. My kindergarten (where I was the youngest one in attendance) was putting on an Easter pageant. Apparently, my acting abilities had not surfaced at this early stage (in fact I may still be waiting) so the adults were trying to decide what role they could let me play in the pageant. After much thought and careful consideration, I was awarded the role of "carrot" in the cabbage patch. Let me tell you that I thought I had died and gone to heaven. This was the most exciting thing that had ever happened to me. I was determined to be the best carrot ever, and I just knew this was going to be the highlight of anything I could possibly ever achieve. Being the "dressed up" carrot became the epitome of creativity for me. I reflect back on that time with great fondness, and it truly helps me keep things in perspective. Channeling my "inner carrot" was a stepping stone into finding my own uniqueness along my creative path. The journey continues even after that early burst of celebrity in the cabbage patch, donning my bright orange carrot costume.

Psychologist Howard Gardner introduced the theory of multiple intelligences that can be described as each of us possessing at least seven measurable intelligences: (1) Logical-Mathematical; (2) Verbal-Linguistic; (3) Spatial-Mechanical; (4) Musical; (5) Bodily-Kinesthetic; (6) Interpersonal-Social; and (7) Intrapersonal (Gelb, M. J., 1998). All of us have some of each of these seven measurable intelligences. You based your career(s) on at least one or two of these. The other intelligences lay dormant. A funny thing will happen as you begin to spark your creativity. These other intelligences—the ones that have been lying dormant—will begin to awaken.

Creative people are an endless resource of ideas. Take Leonardo da Vinci. Mr. da Vinci was accomplished in art, invention, military engineering, science, architecture, and sculpting. Leonardo also "dabbled" in anatomy, botany, and geology and physics. In his unique creativity, Mr. da Vinci practiced seven principles (Gelb, M. J., 1998). Those principles are: (1) having an insatiably curious approach to life and a passion for continuous learning; (2) having a commitment to test knowledge through experience, persistence, and a willingness to learn from mistakes; (3) developing a refinement of the senses, especially sight, as the means to enliven experiences; (4) having a willingness to embrace ambiguity, paradox, and uncertainty; (5) developing a balance between science and art, logic, and imagination; (6) cultivating grace, ambidexterity, fitness, and poise; and (7) recognizing and appreciating the interconnectedness of all things and phenomena or systems thinking (Gelb, M. J., 1998).

Let's take a moment to see how you can develop your da Vinci skills. Fill in short answers in response to the questions in the following table.

Da Vinci's Principles	Example in High School	Example in College	Example from Ages 20-50	Possible *Gap-Time* Examples
Insatiable Curiosity About Life				
Example:	Mixing enough chemicals to cause a small explosion.	Taking a world religions class as an elective.	Training for marathons in five states and planning some vacation time to take in the sights after the race.	Learning new computer software to start the family genealogy.
Test Knowledge Through Experience				
Example:	The shortest distance to the goal is a direct line (through the linebackers).	Working as a student teacher utilizing methods learned as a student.	Creating an IRA and now having six figures.	Volunteer at SCORE to share knowledge and business experience with first-time business owners.
Refinement of Senses				

Example:	Taking a Home Economics class and enjoying the smell of freshly baked cookies.	Sketching with pencils.	Attending performances of the local symphony.	Enjoying Leisure Classes that offer cooking and art.
Working with Ambiguity, Paradox, and Uncertainty				
Example:	Joining the debate team.	Presenting opposing arguments in a law class.	Working on political campaigns.	Assisting others to complete their G.E.D.
Balance Between Science and Art, Logic and Imagination				
Example:	Creating a mobile of the planets, sun, and moon.	Mixing icing in a class to demonstrate a teaching method and then eating the results.	Digital photography of landscapes to decorate the home.	Creating note cards from photographs using various subject themes.
Cultivating Grace, Ambidexterity, Fitness, and Poise				

Example:	Cheerleading.	Learning Ballet.	Participating in Yoga classes.	Playing tennis, golf, and swimming and dancing.
Recognition and Appreciation of Interconnectedness				
Example:	Team sports.	Sororities and Fraternities.	Participating in your church to serve the poor.	Starting a pet visitation program at a nearby veterans home.

Having a degree in mathematics, I have always appreciated and enjoyed logical problem—solving, but most of all delving into the history of mathematicians as it is akin to their deeper philosophical interests and beliefs. Da Vinci's principles have inspired and assisted me through many periods of my life, and I hope that you will embrace these principles throughout your *Gap-Time*.

Dr. Dyer suggests sharing something of yourself on a daily basis with no expectation of being acknowledged or thanked. You may enjoy sending a card to someone who is having a particularly bad day, dropping off canned goods at a local food bank, sending flowers to someone for no particular reason, or sending a King Cake to someone for Mardi Gras. It doesn't matter if what you do is big or small. It only matters that you are beginning your day in a state of gratitude or "in-Spirit" that opens your channels of creativity.

Please take a moment to review some key elements of Chapter 2: your vision statement, the differences between your vision statement and how you are currently living, your obstacles, and the environment in which you feel that you are the natural "you." On a piece of paper, list some techniques to "find" the natural or creative you. But before you list those, let's look at some possible suggestions.

Leonardo da Vinci suggested choosing a "theme for the day" to focus curiosity. Make up 10 questions you have for your theme, record the questions either in a journal or notebook, or on your computer. You can write down your thoughts, make accurate and simple observations, speculate about the topic, offer an opinion on the topic, and research theories on the topic. "Some favorite themes include: Emotions, Seeing, Listening, Touch, Aesthetics, and Animals" (Gelb, M. J., 1998). You could share the same theme with a friend and then compare notes at the end of the day. Make sure that you read all of your notes. What are your insights?

Select three favorite themes that shed the most "optimistic" light on you as a person. With each topic, identify your strengths.

Topic 1: _____

Topic 2: _____

Topic 3: _____

Similarly, Julia Cameron recommends in her book, *The Artist's Way,* a daily practice of early morning writing called "stream-of-consciousness" for long-term change and waking up your inner creativity (Cameron, J., 1992). "In order to retrieve your creativity, you need to find it." She refers to these as "morning pages." Morning pages are crucial in helping to unblock your creativity and free your mind of space. Cameron recommends writing three long-hand pages each morning, totally stream of conscious. "Although occasionally colorful, the morning pages are often negative, frequently fragmented, often self-pitying, repetitive, stilted or babyish, angry or bland—even silly sounding. Good! All that angry, whiny, petty stuff that you have written down in the morning pages stands between you and your creativity." Getting all that negative stuff out of your head and onto a blank page clears your head and frees your mind for more positive things. It allows you to move on. It will appear to be a mind-numbing exercise, but something magical begins to take shape. You begin to connect to your inner voice. Ideas become clear, problems get solved, synchronicity begins to show up at random times in random places. Synchronicity will be discussed in greater detail later in the book.

A number of talented individuals use "stream-of-consciousness" exercises to recover or expand their creativity. Stream-of-consciousness is a method of writing either (1) whatever is on your mind, or (2) in response to a question you have already formulated. Dr. Dyer writes and speaks about awakening early in the morning without the aid of an alarm clock and immediately writing whatever is in his heart or mind. Other individuals choose a question and devote at least 10 minutes to writing responses.

Whatever method you choose, the basic technique is the same. Do not lift your pen from the paper or remove your fingers from the keyboard (long-hand is recommended as it connects you at a deeper level). Do not stop and correct spelling or grammar. Stream-of-consciousness creates a lot of repetitive words, nonsense, and redundancy, but it also sheds light on unique insights and understandings. "There is no wrong way to do morning pages," says Cameron.

Once you complete your writing, take a break. Read the text that you just wrote out loud. Underline or highlight the words or phrases that speak most strongly to you. Do you see a theme? Do you see more questions? Is there the beginning of a book, poem, song, or recipe resonating beside the mental goop you just splattered on the page? Do you see a path for a different vocation or a business?

Roger von Oech suggests the following considerations in awakening creativity:

- "The cosmos speaks to us in patterns;
- A wonderful harmony arises from joining together the seemingly unconnected;
- That which opposes produces a benefit;
- If all things turned to smoke, the nose would be the discriminating organ;
- Lovers of wisdom must open their minds to very many things indeed;
- The most beautiful order is a heap of sweepings piled up at random;
- Those who approach life like a child playing a game moving and pushing pieces, have the kingly power;
- Knowing many things doesn't teach insight;
- On a circle, an end point can also be a starting point;
- The way up and the way down are one and the same;
- A thing rests by changing;
- Many do not grasp what is right in the palm of their hand;
- When there is no sun, we can see the evening stars;

- Expect the unexpected, or you won't find it, because it doesn't leave a trail;
- When we're awake, there is one ordered universe, but in sleep each of us turns away from this world to one of our own; and,
- Your character is your destiny." (von Oech, 1998).

Remember to give yourself permission to be the authentic "you" and to be a beginner in the creativity department. Some bad habits are excusable. Leonardo was criticized for leaving many incomplete works behind. So if you have several incomplete projects, you are in good company. Cut yourself some slack . . . Just keep going!

In testimony to the power of the authentic and creative you, here's a little story. "In December 1945, a farmer near the Egyptian city of Nag Hammadi discovered over 50 scrolls of mystical Coptic writings dating back to 140 A.D. The passages were a collection of sayings of Jesus, some of which are included in the New Testament, and many of which are not. The writings have come to be known as *The Gospel of Thomas*. One of the most compelling of these lessons (paraphrased here) teaches: If you bring forth what is within you, it will save you. If you do not bring forth what is within you, it will kill you" (Cohen, A. H., 2002).

Take what you know to be your true calling and act on it. If not today, then when? You were created for a purpose on this earth. Open the doors and the windows of your creativity to take charge of your future! My Grandmother Fletcher was a true 19th century Renaissance woman—she had a visionary perspective of life, study and love. She graduated with a Bachelor of Science degree in 1894—yes—1894. She became a school principal at a time when women weren't typically given such positions. As if those accomplishments weren't enough, she then married and went on to mother six children, and raise an additional six stepchildren.

Yes—12 kids in all! In her spare time, she wrote poetry under the pseudonym, Annie Rooney.

... let him forsake the low valley and climb the mountains, his vision expands the heavens grow brighter and brighter and he sees more and more of the beautiful sky above. He reaches the summit of some lofty peak, the bright sun and the whole heavens come within his view. He can get a view of valleys, plains and landscapes he never dreamed of before. Stars, planets pass before his eyes that could not be seen while in the valley. So it is in this life, human progress is only developing and refining of the powers originally given us by our Creator.

Grandma Fletcher, a.k.a. Mammy Fletch to her grandkids, may not have consciously mapped out her *Gap-Time* plan, but if she were still around, you can bet she wouldn't be polishing off her rocking chair. I bet we'd find her running for political office or picking up a hobby like sky-diving.

Whether you call it in-Spirit, connectedness, intelligence, or some other name or phrase, the push is to take the information you learned about yourself in Chapter 2, pair it with your areas of creativity identified in Chapter 3, and carry it into the next phase of your *Gap-Time* planning. This is a fun, exciting time. Best of all—it's your time. The only limit to your creativity is you! Explore! Play! Discover! The world awaits . . .

If my heart can become pure and simple like that of a child, I think there probably can be no greater happiness than this.

Kitaro Nishida (The Little Zen Companion)

Chapter 4

Stop playing it safe with employment and life-long learning

> "There is the risk that you cannot afford to take, [and] there is the risk you cannot afford not to take."
> —Peter Drucker

The risk that you cannot afford *not* to take is becoming the authentic you. In the words of Michelangelo, "The greater danger for most of us lies not in setting our aim too high and falling short; but in setting our aim too low, and achieving our mark."

"In my late 40s, I noticed I was beginning to make safer choices in life, shying away from the new and unexplored, sticking to things I already could do well rather than sticking my neck out and trying something difficult.... The way I see it, you've got to fight the conservative impulse that leads you to make ever-saner, more sensible choices. If you don't turn that old phrase, *'better safe than sorry,'* on its head from time to time, the circumference of your life will shrink and shrink . . . . Facing down fear reminds you that you're tough, adventurous, capable" (Cradell, 2007).

Speaking of adventurous, for many semesters I have served as an administrator and lecturer on "Semester at Sea" (*www.semesteratsea.com*). We literally sail around the world for an entire semester—100 days—and circumnavigate the globe (35,000 miles). Could I have ever imagined those many, many years ago when I was standing on that stage as the world's best carrot that one day I'd be sailing around the world pursuing my passion? I thought I'd hit my high point in the cabbage patch, but I steadfastly pursued my passions, and they've carried me around the globe. Eventually, those passions led me right out of that cabbage patch and onto the high seas. Take a risk. If you want to run a marathon, sign up for your first 5-k tomorrow. Dream the impossible dream—go ahead, I dare you.

> To fight the unbeatable foe
> To bear with unbearable sorrow
> To run where the brave dare not go
>
> To right the unrightable wrong
> To love pure and chaste from afar
> To try when your arms are too weary
> To reach the unreachable star
>
> *Lyrics from "The Impossible Dream"*
> *by Joe Darion*

Never mind the stereotypical beliefs that when one retires, one stops working, or living, or dreaming for that matter. Does your *Gap-Time* plan include continued employment? Will that employment be at the same job, but just fewer hours? Will your employment be in a field that is similar to your current work? Or will your employment be in a field totally different from your current job? I think my friend Dianne—you remember Dianne with the midnight blue Jaguar—is the best example of living creatively and taking risks in the *Gap-Time*. Mind you, Dianne has never been an under-achiever, to say the least. In her career, she held various positions within the field of education, including a stint as supervisor of guidance and counseling, Louisiana State Department of Education.

Like many women, she got married and had children. Once her kids got into high school, she realized she wasn't content sitting around the house. Having that passion for education, she realized there were problems in the system and decided to go back to teach. Along that time, she also decided to dip her toes into local politics and became the first woman to hold a City Council seat. After a while, she decided to leave teaching. Not being one to sit still for long—and because her husband needed help at his medical practice—she accepted the role of office manager on a temporary basis and ended up staying 12 years. By that time, they had three kids in out-of-state colleges; so while it may not have been what she planned for, it sure helped with the tuition costs! Her next project was planning her youngest daughter's wedding, which she threw herself into with a vengeance. Once that event passed, she found herself at loose ends, without a project and/or a purpose. It was on a rainy trip to visit her grandkids that that all changed for Dianne.

"We went to visit my daughter and her family. We were staying in a hotel and we had our two grandkids in the room with us as we were planning to take them to a movie. We had a couple of hours to kill, it was raining outside, and the kids were getting antsy. This not being my town, I called my daughter and asked her for some ideas on how to entertain them. She suggested that we take them to this paint-your-own-pottery place nearby, so we did. Our intention was to kill time before the movie, but it was so much fun, we ended up staying all day!" Something clicked with Dianne that day, and she came home and decided to open her own pottery studio. That is exactly what she did, but it gets better. She opened this place—which the town embraced because there was nothing like it anywhere around—but then she started bringing in local artists to teach. One thing leads to another, and Dianne finds herself picking up a paintbrush and learning to paint. Pretty soon, people are buying her work! She has since closed that location and opened up another right in her own backyard. She goes on artists' retreats with her artist friends who call themselves the "Fast and Loose Ladies from New Roads," which has to do with their style of painting, by the way. So here is this woman who not only opens up a successful business, but discovers her inner artist along the way. Dianne is absolutely enjoying life to the fullest and all because a little rain sent her out of her way. That, my friends, is the true essence of *Gap-Time*. She didn't let anything or anyone stand in the way of her vision, and she sure wasn't afraid to take a little risk. "I didn't know enough about what I was doing to know I couldn't do it," says Dianne. Her life went in a whole new direction that she never dreamed possible because she was open to it, and she was having fun. She hasn't totally gotten out of politics either—she's up to her elbows in the 2008 presidential campaign and loving every minute of that, too.

"When I retired from Porter Novelli in 1990 at the age of 49, I had no intention of beginning a life of leisure. I wanted to pursue my goal of making a difference by beginning a new career in public service.... Michael concluded that successful retirement required serious reflection about what really mattered to him, followed by a test-drive of the new life before leaving the old one.

Michael loved his new role as a non-profit business consultant, working with organizations such as the National Institute for Youth Entrepreneurship and a local chapter of 100 Black Men of America, but he also found that he missed the corporate life. So, earlier this year, he went back into the corporate suite as chief human resources officer and senior vice president. Michael's odyssey demonstrates that the road to retirement is not a straight path, but can be filled with twists and turns, which is what makes the journey exciting" (Novelli & Workman, 2006).

Although my friend Dong is years away from retiring, his vision isn't necessarily one of more free time, but rather freedom to use his time more freely. "The best of all possible worlds is to work at something that you enjoy and make a living doing it," says Dong. "The next is to work to support what you enjoy. I see retirement as a promotion in life that gives you the ability to do what you enjoy. If what you enjoy is your career, then continue doing it. If you want to be a kayak guide, then do that. When you enjoy what you are doing, then it's truly 'free time'." I couldn't agree with Dong more. When you realize you have choices and options, it is liberating. Information is power, so arm yourself with information about yourself, and use that information to access your options.

What do you already know how to do, what are you really good at, and what provides your competitive differentiation from others? Most importantly, what fires your flame? What makes your eyes light up at the mere mention? In other words, what is your foundation to act on your vision of a new career and/or passion? Many people forget about their hobbies or their sports interests, or their volunteer work when asked about competencies. Those are the very areas that you may focus employment opportunities on during your *Gap-Time*. Maybe it's something you did a hundred years ago and have long since forgotten or maybe, like Dianne, it's something that you're about to try for the first time. Again—an open mind, a positive attitude and a little creativity will lead you to where you are supposed to be, but most importantly, it will lead you to where you want to be in your *Gap-Time*.

Using the information that you gathered on yourself in the exercises in Chapters 2 and 3, let's identify what your employment options could be. Employment, full-time or part-time, can provide social and mental stimulation as well as a source of income. Take a moment to reflect on your interests and attitudes relative to work after retirement.

- Would you be happier working for yourself or for others?
- Does the idea of being a sole proprietor appeal to you?
- Do you enjoy working alone more than with others?
- Do you prefer working inside or outside?
- Do you enjoy traveling or being on the road for long periods at a time?
- Do you prefer working with machines or with people?
- Do you have a hobby that is salable?
- Have any of your past ventures been successful? If so, what were they?
- Is there a job connected with your education that appeals to you?
- What has been your most rewarding experience?
- Is there a local business that you frequent as a customer that might appeal to you as an employment opportunity, i.e., a coffee shop or boutique?
- Is there a dream lying dormant, i.e., I'd love to own my own café or diner?
- Do you have the resources to finance such a venture?
- Where could you go for additional answers, i.e., Small Business Bureau? Friends?

(Donaho, M.W. & Meyer, J. L., 1976)

Let's try another exercise. Take 60 seconds and quickly write five "dream jobs." Quickly! Don't think about whether or not you have the experience or the education or the skill. Stop thinking and WRITE!

My DREAM jobs are . . .

1)
2)
3)
4)
5)

We're deep sea fishing here to see what we catch. Don't limit your possibilities. Let's just see what is lying below the surface of your conscious brain. Maybe "movie star" came up on your list. While that might be a real possibility, perhaps doing some community theater is an option you hadn't allowed yourself.

I always enjoyed teaching honors students advanced math, but at some point I realized I wanted to explore opportunities in counseling vs. teaching. I went back to school and began taking night classes at Southern Methodist University (SMU) and received my Master's degree in Education/Counseling. As a counselor, about 40 % of my students were from low-income families. Let there be no doubt that many of these kids had the cards stacked against them, but I've never seen anyone work so hard at overcoming issues as they did. Working with these kids remains one of my most rewarding experiences.

There's good news. If you haven't liked what you've been doing, you can change. Barbara Sher, author of *I Could Do Anything If I Only Knew What It Was*, convinces her readers that although we may not know what we want to do, there usually are several "supposed-to" messages that have found their way into our lives (Sher, B., 1994). Unfortunately, some of us have been living the "supposed-to" message

(I was supposed to be married, be an engineer, a lawyer, a doctor, a nurse, a teacher, make money, and live happily ever after) instead of the "want" message that was playing in your head and heart. (I want to be a manager, a veterinarian, a banker, the owner of my own business). So for some of us, we were "imitating" the interests of others and not our own in our employment, and probably elsewhere as well. "To those who do not recognize their unique worth, imitation looms attractive; to those who know their strength, imitation represents an unacceptable compromise" (Cohen, A. H., 2002).

Researchers have shown that satisfying work and complexity of purpose are key measures for keeping the brain alert. Back in the 1960s when women graduated college, there were about two employment areas available: nursing and teaching. Unbelievably for that time, I was offered a position with a management consultant company to become a statistical analyst/consultant, but I turned it down. Both my mother and my grandmother were teachers, which helped me decide my path. While the consultant position seemed incredibly lucrative at the time, I felt I had a purpose and a calling to work in the field of education.

"Tying our work to meeting a deeper meaning is a natural evolution for adults today" (Harkness, H., 1999). Older adults are learning the distinction between job, career, and calling. The word, "job," has a slightly negative meaning, denoting a stable, lifetime work that pays the bills. The term, "career" speaks to the more positive notion of filling a need; making a life, and not just a living. "Calling" has the most positive meaning, indicating work (paid or unpaid) with a deeper purpose or meaning; something felt from your heart. A calling is "life-giving" energy that revives our soul and spirit (Harkness, H., 1999). It's important to note that full-time homemakers are, in fact, unpaid workers who are equipped to multi-task, plan, organize, and budget well beyond the capabilities of some corporate presidents.

As you read in Chapter 3, individuals need the opportunity to express their creativity. Generation X grew up with the idea that they weren't going to just work at a job, they were going to have careers with meaning and purpose. Unfortunately, it's taken our generation a little longer to grasp the concept that work can be fun, and that it can be our calling and not just a paycheck. In our *Gap-Time*, we are no longer "open" to just working at a "job." We are interested in a deeper fulfillment and a greater measure of control over our destiny. Let's take a look at some statistics.

"The trend is national: From 2000 to 2006, the proportion of the nation's 65- to 74-year-olds who remained in the labor force increased from nearly one in five to one in four, according to census figures released this week" (Aizenman, N. C. & Constable, P., 2007, September 14). "Squeezed by soaring health-care costs and dwindling pensions, even more Americans are choosing to postpone retirement—and the Washington, D.C. region leads the nation when it comes to working past age 65, according to census figures released today . . . . But the sharp spike in the percentage of workers 65 and older was the survey's most remarkable finding. Nationally, the share of people 65 to 74 who were still working jumped from one in five in 2000 to one in four in 2006. And the percentage was even higher in the Washington region, where about one-third of people in that age range continued to work" (Washington Post, September 12, 2007).

Ellen Freudenheim states there are five colors of work in retirement. Green is for money and the payment of health costs, products, and services. Red is for heart—some people just love to work and love the work they are doing. Blue is for those who just can't seem to give up working. They are workaholics, and for them work is the continuity in their lives that they crave. Black is for individuals who have a hard time adjusting to change, and retirement represents a serious change. Yellow refers to individuals who receive inspiration and companionship from a job (Freudenheim, E., 2004). What color will you be? Take a quiet moment, close your eyes, and envision yourself in retirement. What do you see? Where are you? What are you doing? What are you wearing? Are you smiling? Take a moment to make a check mark in the column that best describes you now and where you intend to be in three years, in five years, and in 10 years.

	Green: Money and payment of health costs, products and services	Red: Love to work and love the work that I am doing	Blue: Can't give up working	Black: Hard time adjusting to change	Yellow: Receive inspiration and companionship from a job
Today I am:					
In three years I anticipate being:					
In five years I anticipate being:					
In 10 years I anticipate being:					

There are predictions that with so many baby-boomers coming into retirement age, there will be thousands of jobs to fill—which means that *Gap-Timers* would become the new global talent pool. I transitioned out of my career in the federal government into private sector with a consulting company. I soon discovered that I wanted more flexibility in my life so I started my own consulting company. If I can do it, so can you. A dear colleague of mine, who also had been a dean of students, was experiencing academia burnout so he switched coasts and opened up a card shop. I've advised many, many talented educators, who were also experiencing burnout, to take their talents out of a traditional classroom, and put them to use in a different locale—maybe a ship or a corporate classroom. The trick here is to think out of the box—who knows you might end up in a boat! Your skills are transferrable, so get that passport renewed!

What about going back to school? There are hundreds of "leisure" courses designed for mature adults to expand their brain and/or perhaps start on a different career path altogether. A yoga class at the "Y" might lead to a second career as a yoga instructor. A knitting class at the community center might resurrect a long-lost passion that leads to a table at your neighborhood craft show selling your highlysought-after scarves. A deep-sea-fishing trip with your grandson might have you out shopping for a boat to lead your own charters. Heck—you may even find yourself learning on a ship on the ocean, in a cabin on top of a mountain, or in a villa in Italy. Go for it. "Researchers (Chopra, 1993; Restak, 1997; Schaie, 1996) seem to agree that of all the factors contributing to successful brain functioning in the later years, education may be the most important" (Harkness, H., 1999). "Someone once said that 'Education is not merely filling up the pail—it's lighting a fire'" (Heidrich, R. E., 2005).

These "leisure" courses are offered by a host of agencies, educational institutions, and medical facilities on very specific topics. Want to know how to sail a boat? Check with the local Parks and Recreation Department. Want to learn how to use that spreadsheet application on your computer? Look to vocational technical facilities, junior colleges, or even senior centers. Want to learn about glaucoma? Check out the topics offered by your local hospitals. Don't want to leave your house to enroll in a course? Register and take your class online. There are hundreds of online courses offered at campuses around the country, so don't limit yourself to "local" opportunities.

When the time challenge is removed in your *Gap-Time*, you now have the minutes, hours, resources, and energy to pursue topics of interest to you. One couple enrolled in an associate degree program to become registered nurses. They had successful careers prior to retirement but wanted to give back more to the community through nursing—a total departure from their previous employment and educational disposition.

At every turn, there is an opportunity to learn something. I often drop into convention centers when I find myself with extra time on my hands. If there is an exhibition of interest, I will pay the typically small admission fee to check it out. These little excursions have taught me about the latest computer technology, allowed me to demo a Blackberry™, and introduced me to some great authors. If you're fortunate enough to live in a city where you have access to museums, you have a gold mine of learning opportunities at your feet. There's nothing better than discovering a new artist on a rainy day. Maybe the Artrain USA (*www.artrainusa.org*) is in town. If you've never seen this traveling art museum, check it out. If you happen to live in an area that isn't a cultural Mecca, don't let that hinder your adventurous nature. Take up surfing—internet surfing that is! Explore artists via virtual museums and galleries, research the latest technology, and dig up info on your favorite historical figures—all from the comforts of your own home.

Make learning a life-long, as well as a life-time, goal. There is no excuse not to learn. If you're feeling nervous about your upcoming *Gap-Time*, chances are it's because you haven't taken the time to educate yourself on the endless possibilities that lie before you. Educate yourself. Knowledge is power, and regardless of what your hairdresser might say—it is the easiest, best, and perhaps least expensive, way to stay young.

> When the way comes to an end, then change—having changed, you pass through.
>
> I Ching (The Little Zen Companion)

Chapter 5

Relationships and finding social connections

"Shoot for the moon. Even if you miss it, you will land among the stars."

—Les Brown

So far your *Gap-Time* plan has focused solely on you, but that's about to change. While you need to discover (or re-discover) the "you" of you, you also need to take into careful consideration the people currently around you, and the people you want to seek out in your *Gap-Time*. "As we age, we find that social relationships might change. Our preferences in people might change, our interests may change, and we're always gaining new perspectives. What doesn't change is that we still need social structure" (Heidrich, R. E., 2005). Social structure includes our home, family, and friends—and not necessarily in that order.

"Sociologist Robert Weiss found that relationships tend to be specialized in what they provide, and, as a consequence, we need to maintain a number of different relationships for our well-being" (Schlossberg, N., 2004). Six such types of relationships include attachment, social integration, opportunity for nurturance, reassurance of worth, sense of reliable alliance, and obtaining guidance.

Attachment includes relationships that are constant and safe, such as marriage, partnerships, or very close friendships. *Social integration* usually occurs when people work towards a common goal either at work or in a volunteer setting. *Opportunity for nurturance* is our nurturing others, such as friends, family, or children. Those relationships allow us to feel needed. *Reassurance of worth* includes relationships that provide affirmation of our good work either by family or community members. *Sense of reliable alliance* refers to our families—adult children, grandchildren, parents. These are the relationships that have given us roots to grow. *Obtaining guidance* is any relationship that gives advice and good counsel when sought. It infers that some long-time experience has established a level of trust derived from previous guidance (Schlossberg, N., 2004).

I would add a seventh relationship category of *intellectually stimulating* relationships. These folks would be the people who challenge your thoughts and opinions—the people who make you think. Perhaps you are intellectually stimulated by a teacher, a neighbor, or a co-worker. These people undoubtedly are knowledgeable about and ignite a passionate subject for you—perhaps art, the opera, astrology, etc. The fun in these types of relationships is that you can find so many topics that broker different individuals' interests. It's exciting to have conversations with people who are experts in their fields. As my Mom used to say, "I might not be that smart, but I sure do like to be around smart people!" In truth, Mom was really bright, and she'd be the first one educating herself about money matters and reading the newspaper to keep up on current events. Exercising your brain is one of the best investments you can make in your future. Without intellectual stimulation, you become stymied. When your brain becomes inactive, so do you. This inactivity will cause you to suffer greatly, both emotionally and physically. Learning keeps you young. Connecting with others while learning is better than the fountain of youth.

Many of us have spent or are spending at least eight hours of every workday away from home responding to the requirements and demands of our jobs. At retirement you could possibly—assuming you do not elect to work full-time—spend all your waking hours in the same place that you slept and with someone you know all too well. There's an adjustment period with retirement. There are also combinations of adjustments depending upon who retired first, if both retired at the same time, or if one never worked outside the home.

"When I finally retired, it was difficult for both of us in the beginning. Since he had retired first, he came and went on his own. After I retired, I found myself questioning where he was going, what time he would be back, and so on. And if I sat down to do the crossword puzzle in the morning, he would ask me if I was 'going to do anything' that day. That irritated me. It was my time, and if I wanted to do the crossword puzzle, that was up to me! It took awhile to adjust to being together so much of the time. I had to reinforce that the kitchen was my territory, and I was the boss there. Often, he would come into the kitchen and ask what I was doing, why was I doing it that way, and so on. After a while, I would go down to his shop in the basement and ask what he was doing and why he was doing it that way! He soon got the message" (Waxman, B. & Mendelson, R. A., 2006).

Some couples reverse roles when one or both retire. "I basically took over the housework, so that when she came home there was nothing for her to do. Her job became easier because she knew that she didn't have to do the vacuuming and waste weekends on chores. There are no sexist roles here. Why can't I pick up a mop? Being retired, it's my time to take care of the fort" (Waxman, B. & Mendelson, R. A., 2006).

There are special considerations when one is the stay-at-home Mom. "My husband always wanted to know what I was doing. He wanted to organize my day, and then reorganize it. The trick is to not tell him your plans!" (Waxman, B. & Mendelson, R. A., 2006)

My Dad enjoyed a successful career in banking for over 40 years. He retired at the age of 65, and was suddenly at home every day with my Mom. After about 30 minutes of relaxing and enjoying his retirement, he began to educate us all in the time management and operational efficiency skills he had honed over the years at the bank. He taught my mom how to shave minutes off her vacuuming time. He had us re-arranging the kitchen cabinets to increase our productivity when setting the table and putting away the dishes. When he unveiled our "daily schedule," which would clearly make us all better people, Mom quietly slipped into another room and called their mutual friend, Bob, who was president of another bank about 50 miles from where we lived. Within a week, Dad was offered a position as vice president of Public Relations that had just become available at Bob's bank. Dad accepted the job, and needless to say, life leveled out. Mom obviously knew she had to make some *Gap-Time* provisions of her own. They were married for over 50 years, and I'm convinced that their successful union was in large part due to their ability to adjust and re-adjust their schedules.

It's important for couples to sit down and discuss their *Gap-Time* plan for life after retirement. Two key areas to plan for are household roles and how much time you plan to spend together. "All other things being equal, a healthy relationship makes for a healthy retirement; an 'OK' relationship makes for an 'OK' retirement; while a chronically sick relationship makes for a disaster" (Johnson, R. P., 2001). Note: If your relationship falls in the latter category, you probably don't want to wait until your *Gap-Time* to address it.

Examine current relationships to see if you may need to foster new ones to carry you into your *Gap-Time*. Write short answers in the table below to inventory your current relationships.

Relationships Categories	Who Are They In Your Life?	Do I Need to Add, Subtract, or Change in this Relationship Category?
Attachment *Constant and Safe—Marital partners, partners and/or close friends*		
Social Integration *Working toward a common goal—co-workers and peers*		
Opportunity for Nurturance *Who we nurture—friends, family and children*		
Reassurance of Worth *People who reaffirm our good work*		

Sense of Reliable Alliance *People we're connected to who've helped us grow*		
Obtaining Guidance *Those who give us counsel and advice*		
Intellectually Stimulating *Who makes us think? Who challenges our thoughts and opinions of the world?*		

Gap-Timers have a deep emotional need to connect at deep levels with their spouse, friends, or confidantes. Intimacy levels can be rekindled. For couples, *Gap-Time* gives you time to focus on the finer points of romance and the finer points of one's partner, the reasons you fell in love with him or her in the first place. Start "dating" again. He asks her out. She accepts. He plans where they are going, what they will do, and pays for the evening, lunch, or golf date. Then she asks him out. He accepts. She plans where they are going, what they will do, and pays for the date. Okay, so some of you are old-fashioned. He pays for this, too. Bed and breakfast (B&B) getaways in the middle of the week will cost less and provide you with the excitement of getting away. Stay at a B&B in a town or state that you have not visited before. Make it mysterious and fun by visiting at least one "tourist" spot in that town—whether it is a museum, an art gallery, the worlds' largest collection of string, the local winery, or the local cheese maker. Get out and explore.

Find an activity that the two of you enjoy doing and include that in either daily or weekly activities. If you don't have an activity, take one of Leonardo da Vinci's principles and draw from a previous selection of topics and talk through the exercise. There is some truth to the statement that conversation is a lost art mostly because we are too busy to practice it.

Enjoying physical intimacy does not retire when you do. "My father told me all about the birds and the bees—the liar. I went steady with a woodpecker until I was 21"—Bob Hope (Hansen, M. V. & Linkletter, A, 2006). One of the most disingenuous stereotypes surrounding age is that seniors and sex don't mix. "'People don't lose their passion,' one senior says. 'They don't lose wanting to be held, to be touched, having physical contact with another human being (Volz, 2000).'" In a survey published in the *New England Journal of Medicine* in August 2007, scientists are reporting that the sex lives of seniors aged 57 to 85 overturns the notion that physical pleasure is just something for young people (Marchione, 2007). While the interest in sex may diminish, healthier individuals were nearly twice as likely to be sexually active than those in poor or fair health. Not attached to anyone? "Look up an old friend or flame. We all have mysteries in our background—those once-rich relationships that broke up in a flash of temper, or just whispered away. Locate him/her on Google or *Classmates.com*, and reconnect with your past. Perhaps there is a romance ready to be rekindled (Crandell, 2007).

Caring for other family members may be part or become part of your *Gap-Time* plan. For some of us, we may actually delay retirement while others (children, grandchildren, siblings, or parents) are dependent upon us. Many *Gap-Timers* are faced with parenting another generation, their grandchildren, or even their parents in poor health. "In a study by the Pew Research Center, some interesting caregiving statistics emerge . . . . Consider these numbers: 68% of boomers (born between 1946 and 1964) help their adult children financially; 29% of boomers help their parents financially; 13% of boomers help both their adult children *and* their parents financially; 66% of boomers feel parental responsibility for children's college bills; 33% provide housing for adult children; and 56% provide housing for elder parents" (Johnson, R. P., 2006). One courageous *Gap-Timer* opened a company focusing on companionship/assistance for the elderly/infirmed after she finished nursing her own mother through a long illness. She realized the importance of having a caring, trustworthy person available at one's bedside when a family member or friend isn't available.

When you consider retirement, what additional responsibilities do you expect to shoulder from children, grandchildren, siblings, or parents? What options have you included or dismissed because of these parenting or financial challenges?

Stereotypical descriptions of grandparents are out-the-window. "When I was a kid, grandmothers had short, gray hair frozen into a corona of permanent-wave frizz. They stayed home, cooking and cleaning in an extremely unflattering article of clothing we actually called a housedress. Grandfathers went to work and spent weekends slouched in front of the TV, watching the ballgame; grandchildren were beloved but seldom played with. Gramp patted you on the head when you visited and, if you were lucky, slipped a crisp dollar bill into your pocket. Boomer grandparents are a whole new breed. Twenty-first century grandmas wear "skinny" jeans, and they fit grooming appointments—manicures, hair color treatments, even Botox injections—between business meetings. Boomer granddads are as likely to play a pick-up game of basketball as a round of golf. Furthermore, this generation's men are hands-on grandparents, competing with their wives for babysitting assignments" (Cradell, 2007).

"Now that I am retired, I take care of my two grandsons three days a week. I couldn't bear to think of them going to day care.

I enjoy having them around. I was working when my kids were growing up. It's nice to be able to relax and play with them" (Waxman, B. & Mendelson, R. A., 2006). If you do not live close to either your children or your grandchildren, email can maintain that connectedness between face-to-face visits. Even sharing photographs has become easier and quicker now that we no longer have to wait for the U.S. Postal Service to deliver them.

I'm not sure I could handle the circumstances in the next story, but it is becoming more and more common. "We have neighbors who were recently married in their 60s, each with grown children and grandchildren. They went on their honeymoon right after the wedding. Literally the day they returned—and without any warning—the new bride's godchild (a great-niece) was dropped on their doorstep, and they were named the sole custodians. As retirees, they were plopped right back into the life of elementary schools, homework, sleepovers, and kids! At times it's overwhelming, but we also see how much they are in love and how they make the best out of having a surprise family so late in life" (Waxman, B. & Mendelson, R. A., 2006).

Parents and siblings round out this discussion. Elderly parents and their health and financial issues could deal you a wild card. Their longevity and financial resources may impact your financial and emotional state. Make sure you know your parents' financial business the older that they become. If they do not have a will, it's time to discuss one or at least a power-of—attorney over certain business affairs. Without a "Living Will," hospitals and nursing homes are legally bound to provide life-giving support even if your parents have given oral directions to the contrary.

I was a caretaker from afar when my Mom was diagnosed with cancer. I happened to be living 250 miles away, and went home nearly every weekend. It was difficult to manage a full-time job and a household, all while trying to respond to medical conditions and the travel that was required. After a few months of this back-and-forth life, I had to sit back and do some serious evaluating. Should I quit my job and move home? Should I make other caretaker arrangements and entrust my dear Mother's care to someone else? Would I be able to sleep at night? These were all heavy decisions that weighed on me, the only child. It was an incredibly stressful time. It ended up that Mom passed away before I had a chance to decide. No one wants to think of death, but you will not regret having a discussion(s) with your loved ones about their choices and desires. Chances are they've given it some thought.

Siblings should be stable without calling on you for help. But again, there are extreme circumstances shared by retirees that blend stories of the unforeseen. One example is the developmentally disabled sibling who is living with your aged parents. The care of that individual once parents are deceased may impact your *Gap-Time* plan. I believe accounting for the remote possibilities builds flexibility into your retirement. A plan without flexibility is nothing more than a fantasy.

Another scenario is that you and your spouse spent many hours dreaming and planning for your retirement, and those plans go up in smoke due to a divorce. "With a high divorce rate, some people over 55 years of age are simultaneously facing retirement and living alone for the first time in what may seem like eons" (Freudenheim, E., 2004). The key to improving existing relationships and gaining new relationships is connectedness. Connectedness can stem from co-workers; classmates; civic, alumni, or fraternal organizations; church; book clubs; yoga, cooking, or other classes and workshops; tennis or golf lessons; and many other social interactions.

The myth is that the older you get, the harder it is to make friends. The truth is that it's not harder to make friends. The hard part is getting yourself into different venues and situations where you can make connections. If you follow your own hobbies and passions, you'll meet people with common interests which therefore give you a stepping stone upon which to establish a friendship. The key is to develop social relationships that allow you to experience your passions in life.

In Rodney Rothman's book, *Early Bird: A Memoir of Premature Retirement*, the author interviews retired persons living in Florida. "So is retirement what you expected?" "It's hard when you first get here . . . , especially if you're alone like I was." Rothman's questions continued, "Do you have any advice . . . about how to get through the early days? How to adjust faster?" "Well . . . it helps if you find some common interests with people." (Rothman, R., 2006)

What interests do you have? Do you know how to seek out opportunities to interact with others having similar interests? Start by telling your buddies/family/friends about your interests and ask them to notify you when they happen upon information in one of the interest areas you have identified. If you love photography, write down the names of persons you know you could interact with who have the same interest. If you enjoy hiking, write down the names of people that you know who hike and with whom you would enjoy spending time.

When you attend a class, let's say on cooking, ask other students if they would like to keep in touch to share recipes and to notify each other when other cooking classes are offered. Keep and distribute that information among those interested parties, and then you will have a "new" group of friends who share a similar interest with you. Now that I have found time to pursue more interests, I've discovered a love for photography which is a great compliment to my love of travel. Having traveled over five million miles to 70 different countries, I've been able to snap some fabulous pictures. At some point, I even got the confidence to enter some contests, and much to my surprise, I won some awards. As much as I enjoy shooting pictures, I enjoy taking photography classes and meeting different people who share my interest. Besides meeting really interesting people, I always walk away with some great photography tips!

I also belong to a few private clubs, which I've found to be an excellent source for making new friends as well as business resources. It's interesting because many of these relationships start out as friends, then we discover a common business connection, and they evolve into mutually beneficial business relationships, or vice-versa. The subject of "social networking" is probably deserving of its own chapter—or even book—given its newfound gravity. I happen to enjoy going to networking events—and if you live in a large city like I do—you never know whom you're going to be rubbing elbows with. In Washington, D.C., I've found myself standing next to George Clooney, Michael Jordan, Harrison Ford, and many others. The best part, thanks to my love of photography, is that I'm always armed with a camera so I've got the pictures to prove it! Not too bad, huh? Many people think they aren't good networkers and turn down invitations.

"I just don't have the gift of gab," or "I'm just too shy," are common excuses in avoiding the networking scene. Like anything else, social networking takes practice. You have to step out of your comfort zone a few times in order to build your confidence. Remember—everyone else in the room is probably feeling the same insecurities. Relax and enjoy the moment. Be genuine. Be yourself. Listen. When all else fails, keep in mind that everyone likes to talk about themselves. Ask questions. Listen intently to their answers in order to come up with follow-up questions. Look for a common denominator, i.e., something the two of you might have in common. Maybe your children went to the same high school or perhaps you both lived in California during the 1980s. Listen to the details.

You will also need to identify activities that you will do by yourself, such as reading or working out at the gym. Perhaps you enjoy quiet times and want to reserve walks through museums and art galleries for being reflective. "I enjoy a leisurely cup of coffee," says Mary. "When I was busy making a living and raising kids, I would dash out of the house gulping down a cup of coffee. Having time to spend enjoying a leisurely cup of coffee is such a pleasure." Take advantage of your quiet time. Slow down and enjoy the simple things in life that we take for granted on a daily basis—a hot bath, the newspaper, a leisurely chat with a neighbor, or a stroll in the park. Remember those busy days when you had three kids tied to your apron strings after a long day at the office or too many responsibilities to even think about an attitude adjustment day? You would have killed for a day of peace and quiet. What did you dream of doing with your private time? Sometimes when you have that quiet time, it's hard to think of what to do because you're overly focused on being alone.

We will focus on identifying activities that you will want to do with others and activities that you will want to do alone (usually). Transfer the information you completed in Chapter 2 of all the "Areas of Importance that I plan to keep or to attain five to 10 years from now." You can also add some new activities. Place those topics in the Table below and then check appropriate columns.

Area of Importance that I plan to keep or to attain 5 to 10 years from now (that scored either a 4 or a 5)	Activities with others	Activities just for me	Activities that could be either with others or by myself
Activity: _____			
Activity: _____			
Activity: _____			
Activity: _____			
Activity: _____			

Activity: _____			
Activity: _____			
Activity: _____			
Activity: _____			
Activity: _____			
Activity: _____			
Activity: _____			
Activity: _____			
Activity: _____			

Keep a list of things you'd like to do and/or explore when you have the time. If you're finding yourself with a lot of extra time on your hands, you're going to want to pay special attention to Chapter 7.

Whatever interests, is interesting.

William Hazlitt (The Little Zen Companion)

Chapter 6

Healthy concerns

"To keep the body in good health is a duty.... Otherwise we shall not be able to keep our mind strong and clear."

—Buddha

"Health is like oxygen in that you tend not to notice it until it's no longer there" (Heidrich, R. E., 2005). While television, radio, newspaper and magazine ads draw your attention to "fixing" your appearance, physicians recommend a combined physical routine that includes attention to endurance, strength, balance, and flexibility (Freudenheim, E., 2004). Perhaps one of the most vocal proponents of senior health is Jack LaLanne. Some of you may recall that LaLanne had an exercise television show that aired throughout the country in the 1950s.

Mr. LaLanne demonstrated a number of exercise routines and also made recommendations for healthy eating. Mr. La Lanne celebrated his 93rd birthday on September 26, 2007, and is still known as the "Godfather of Fitness."

LaLanne opened the nation's first modern health studio in 1936 after he spent a number of years transforming his life and his body away from sugar, snacks, and flab toward healthy, fit, trim, and muscular. LaLanne developed a basic approach to physical fitness and proved that a healthy diet and systematic exercise are the principle keys to a longer, healthier life. When people lose the physical ability to do things on their own, it's more likely because they have become inactive as they've grown older. One philosophy of LaLanne's is that people don't die of old age, they die of inactivity. So what can you do to stay active?

Carefully evaluate advertisements. "Quick fix" programs rarely work—you know the ones that promise a physique like Mr. or Ms. America within a week or two. Folks starting such a program are often disappointed and give up shortly after starting. Just like the tortoise in the *Tortoise and the Hare*, "nice and easy" tends to promote sustained activity, thus achieving the goal.

Experts indicate that changing one's lifestyle requires thought, planning, and several tries before there is a "permanent" change in behavior. How do you get started?

First, you can identify the activities that you enjoy and/or do as a part of your weekly routine. Second, obtain information about those physical activities. For instance, if you play golf, learn about the muscles used in that activity. If vacuuming the house is part of your weekly routine, learn about the different sets of muscles required to perform that activity. If you do nothing, what are the consequences?

Write down the activities you know you will continue doing. Label those activities according to the form of exercise. There are two forms of exercise that are generally recognized: that of lifestyle activity and that of structured exercise (Ettinger, W. H., Wright, B. S. & Blair, S. N., 2006).

Lifestyle exercise includes vacuuming, gardening, working in the yard, taking brisk walks to do errands, taking the stairs instead of the elevators, and many more examples that you have probably thought of while reading these. Structured exercise is what LaLanne promotes, i.e., the stretching and conditioning of each set of muscles throughout the body. A combination of both types of exercise promotes optimal health.

To your list of activities, add five additional activities that you are *not* currently doing, but would consider doing if given some motivation to do so. By each one of those activities, write three motivations that would stimulate you to incorporate that activity into your weekly routine. Did you list "others," such as activities with family or friends as part of your motivations? Having a support system in place is proven to be one of the most effective impacts for the overall success of continued healthy behavior.

Activities Table

Current Lifestyle Activities Ex: Vacuuming, Gardening, etc.	Motivating Factors	People You Could Enjoy Them With
1)		
2)		
3)		
4)		
5)		

Current Structured Exercise Ex: Tennis	Motivating Factors	People You Could Enjoy Them With
1)		
2)		
3)		
4)		
5)		
Activities/Exercises I'd Like to Try	Motivating Factors	People You Could Enjoy Them With
1)		
2)		
3)		
4)		
5)		

Next, create a written physical activity plan for the next four weeks. Each day, record which activities you completed. Identify and write down other activities that you completed that were not on your list and determine whether or not it is one that you would want to continue in future weeks. At the end of four weeks, review the information that you have written down. Develop your activity plan for the following four weeks. Follow the same procedures for noting activities completed and new activities. Repeat the evaluation process. Complete this process for one more four-week period. At the conclusion of the third set, you should have a plan that is workable for the rest of the year.

Experts recommend determining your current physical limitations and building an exercise plan around those limitations, but also developing a "Phase II" exercise plan that gets you around those limitations to a new level of improved physical movement. Most fitness plans start with stretching and specific activities intended to improve cardio function. A sample exercise plan might look like this:

Stretching would include back, neck, shoulder, elbow, shin, foot, legs, and calves.

Day of the Week	Activity
Sunday	Window-shop in center city or walk the mall.
Monday	Swim or use elliptical for 30 minutes.
Tuesday	Take a three-mile walk with a friend.
Wednesday	Use work-out video tape for 30 minutes.
Thursday	Play tennis or use exercise bike for 30 minutes.
Friday	Take a 3-mile walk with a friend.
Saturday	Gardening and Housework.

Consult your physician before starting any exercise program.

As previously mentioned, I was an avid tournament tennis player and skier. I love physical exercise. As my body aged, my physical limitations increased, and kept me from participating as much as I had previously enjoyed. A few years back, I enlisted the help of a personal trainer, Richard. Richard created a workout for me that was geared specifically to my needs and goals. He charted my progress and switched up my workout as needed to keep me challenged. Working out with Richard gave me the confidence to keep going on my own and helped me to realize what my "real" limitations were vs. my "perceived" limitations, which were huge for me. I didn't think I was capable of some things physically, but Richard wasn't buying it. Additionally, I had a pretty major back surgery many years ago so I have to be careful of some exercises, but Richard pushed me, and surprisingly (to me) I didn't crumble. After a while, I began to challenge myself more and more. I'm not taking on tennis challenges or skiing black-diamond slopes, but I am doing a lot more things. Where the body is concerned, an open mind and positive "can do" attitude is key. You'll be surprised at what you can train (or re-train) the body to do. It is truly a miraculous machine.

If you have a particular health concern that limits a full range of bodily motion, such as arthritis, osteoporosis, or diabetes, you should take a little more care to identify activities that do not aggravate the condition or trigger symptoms. For instance, swimming uses most major muscle groups, and is also a non-impact, non-weight-bearing exercise. Several years ago, I was diagnosed with an arthritis condition, which was difficult to for me to accept. I was prescribed medication which helped, but was told that exercise would be imperative. Some days are better than others, but I know staying active is key to my continued health and mobility. For those without health limits, you should explore all types of physical exercise. That's where the real fun begins.

Re-popularized by the television show *Dancing with the Stars*, one recommended form of exercise that combines all areas of activity is dancing. Alternate fast-paced dances (jitterbug, samba, fox trot) with slower dances (waltzes). By the way, this is an excellent way to make new social connections—sign up for a salsa class and see how many friends you make. Before you declare you have two left feet, there are a number of other exercises you can follow. Walking is also an excellent cardio workout, and studies show that you can benefit from as little as 10 minutes a day. Time spent at the local gym on cardio equipment, playing tennis, and swimming are all excellent vehicles for keeping physically active.

"When the first Marine Corps Marathon took place in 1976, the oldest runner to finish the 26.2 mile race was 58 years old. On the race's 30th anniversary, the oldest finisher was 82—one individual's testament to how Americans are aging differently than they used to" (Washington Post, September 12, 2007). "Physical activity is not an all-or-nothing proposition" (Freudenheim, E., 2004). Check with your doctor before you start any new exercise program.

Diet is a major factor in obtaining and maintaining optimal health. "If the humane society could rescue people who abuse their bodies like they rescue abused pets, a lot of us would find ourselves in animal shelters" (Cohen, A. H., 2002). Numbers mean more than just your age when contemplating optimal health. Your waist size, your Body Mass Index (BMI), and your cholesterol level are just a few examples. We are not striving for Barbie™ and Ken™ figures but according to Drs. Roizen and Oz, women should have a waist size no larger than 32 ½ inches, and men no larger than 35 inches (Roizen, M. F. & Oz, M. C., 2006). The basis of these recommendations is that the larger your waist size, the more likely you are to endanger your health.

You can also evaluate your state of health by calculating your BMI. All you need is your weight (in pounds) and your height (in inches). To calculate your BMI, figure your height in inches then multiply that number by itself. For instance, if you are 5 feet in height, you are 60 inches tall. The next step is to multiply that number by itself (60 x 60 = 3600). Divide your weight (let's assume you weigh 130 pounds) by the number generated from multiplying your height by itself (130/3600 = .03611). Take the resulting number (.03611) and multiply that number by 703 (.03611 x 703 = 25.4). The resulting number is your BMI. A BMI of 18.5-24.9 is normal. A BMI of 25.0-29.9 is considered overweight. A BMI of 30.0 or more is considered obese (Heidrich, R. E., 2005). Physicians and weight control experts use the BMI chart as a range of weights that indicate underweight, average weight, overweight and obese categories for your height. BMI is also used as a predictive tool for risks of obesity to your health (Roizen, M. F. & Oz, M. C., 2006).

To promote healthy living in your *Gap-Time*, an increased focus on nutrition will serve you well. It's important to maintain your activity level to handle your caloric intake. When your BMI strays into the overweight or obese category, you need to consider some corrective actions (increasing activity and lowering caloric intake).

Many of us need some assistance from time to time to get back into the "healthy" range of weight. There are vast numbers of diets, diet aids, diet books, diet clinics, and even surgery to assist you, but buyer, beware. Unfortunately, most diets don't "reprogram" you to think or to develop a new lifestyle to support changes that are made. What that means is that in a matter of time, you revert back to old habits and behaviors (Roizen, M. F. & Oz, M. C., 2006). That especially goes for programs with prepared meals. When you stop purchasing pre-made meals without modifying your initial behaviors, the weight usually returns. The results are the same as if you had stopped any diet and resumed pre-diet behaviors. Usually, you will not only regain the weight you lost, but add a few more pounds.

Just like exercise, the more successful lifestyle changes with regard to diet are accomplished when there is accountability either between you and a family member, friend or a support group. There are a number of those resources available to you. For more information on diets and exercising in the *Gap-Time*, the National Institute on Aging, the AARP, and the Center for Disease Control (CDC) are all good resources.

Health concerns include mental fitness in your *Gap-Time* assessment. One elderly grandmother was visited by the pastor of her church during which time he inquired if she had any concerns. She volunteered that she had a lot of concerns about the hereafter. The pastor consoled her by saying she had lived a good life, was a shining example to her children, and had many more attributes, assuring her that she shouldn't worry about the hereafter. "You don't understand," she said. "I go to the refrigerator, open the door and wonder what I am here after. I go to the cupboard, open the door and wonder what I am here after." We all have "senior" moments. That's one reason why we should learn how to exercise our minds. Malnutrition of the brain is serious. Just like my personal trainer, Richard, helped me with my physical exercise, perhaps we should hire brain trainers. Like your biceps, your mind has to be exercised daily or else it will turn to jelly.

What happens to your brain as you get older? Many people assume that mental and physical abilities necessarily decline with age; that we are, after age 25, losing significant brain capacity on a daily basis. Actually, the average brain can improve with age (Gelb, M. J., 1998). Marilyn Albert (cited in Restak, 1997) of Massachusetts General Hospital and Harvard Medical School has tested thousands of older people over two decades. She has discovered four factors associated with enhanced brain function and healthy brain aging, of which she believes self-efficacy to be the most important:

- "Education—produces neuronal connections;
- Strenuous exercise—increases blood and oxygen supply to brain by maintaining the health of the blood vessels connecting heart to brain;
- Enhanced lung function—increases oxygen in blood stream from lungs to brain;
- Self-efficacy—taking control of one's life and destiny. (Harkness, H., 1999).

Social interaction with others is another excellent form of brain exercise (Heidrich, R. E., 2005). The ways to meet and interact with others are as varied as there are numbers of people. Examples of those activities were provided in Chapter 5.

Exercising the brain can very likely delay Alzheimer's disease symptoms for years (Harkness, H., 1999). Educated individuals are less likely to show symptoms of Alzheimer's as well. Intellectual activity develops brain tissue that later can compensate for tissue damaged by Alzheimer's disease. The brain is like a muscle; the more you use it, the better it works. "Researchers (Chopra, 1993; Restak, 1997; Schaie, 1996) seem to agree that of all the factors contributing to successful brain functioning in the later years, education may be the most important" (Harkness, H., 1999). Other researchers have indicators that show satisfying work and complexity of purpose as key measures for keeping the brain alert.

Before we leave the topic of health, let's take a look at spirituality and health. Several studies show a link between spirituality and longevity. A Duke University study showed that older people who regularly attended religious services had lower levels of interleukin-6, a protein linked to immune system diseases, including lupus, rheumatoid arthritis, and B-cell lymphoma. A Dartmouth Medical School study concluded that patients with an active social life and a strong religious faith were less likely to die in the six months after heart surgery. Frequent churchgoers are more likely to live longer than people who do not attend services frequently, according to another study. A study conducted in 2005 found that individuals aged 65 and older who attended church once per week had a 32 % lower mortality rate than those individuals who did not attend church (Hansen, M. V. & Linkletter, A., 2006).

"In a survey conducted by the National Council on Aging, two out of every three people over 65 rated spirituality as very important in having a meaningful, vital life.... notes a shift from a spirituality defined by geography—a specific house of worship in a specific neighborhood—to a 'spirituality of seeking,' which includes art and music, personal reflection, encounters with the sacred, and development of the inner self" (Freudenheim, E., 2004).

- Do your *Gap-Time* plans include time for exercise?
- What physical activities would you like to pursue?
- Will you join a gym?
- Will you hire a personal trainer?
- How will your diet improve/change in your *Gap-Time*?
- What actions can you take to discover a more healthy you?
- Have you had a physical in the last year?
- What is your BMI?
- Is there a friend or family member who can be your "health" partner?
- What are you doing to exercise your brain?

- Do you enjoy a spiritual life?
- Do you spend time in quiet reflection?
- What are your religious/spiritual beliefs?
- How will you embrace them in your *Gap-Time*?

When making your choice in life, do not neglect to live.

Samuel Johnson (The Little Zen Companion)

Chapter 7

Volunteer, be all you can be!

"With courage you will dare to take risks, have the strength to be compassionate and the wisdom to be humble. Courage is the foundation of integrity."
—Keshavan Nair

Gap-Time empowers us to take charge of our lives and our time. Your avocation may become your vocation. "The United States has one of the most educated work forces—and therefore, soon will boast one of the most educated older populations—in the world. Count among them legions of lawyers; doctors; educators; engineers; managers, financiers and bankers; nonprofit executives; sales, marketing, and communications professionals; and small business owners. All these people—all this talent—collectively spending light years on the golf course?

Unlikely! In the decades ahead, there will probably be an explosion of social entrepreneurial activities, as people find their own ways to make the world a better place" (Freudenheim, E., 2004).

As President John F. Kennedy so eloquently said, "Ask not what your country can do for you; ask what you can do for your country." If helping the whole country seems too overwhelming, how about replacing the word "country" with church, Red Cross, animal shelter, nursing home, etc. The Kennedys and Shrivers have provided us great examples of dedication to serving the needs of others. As *Gap-Timers*, we've acquired the skills to really make a difference, and every one of us has the power to make a difference.

"When I left the White House, I knew I wanted to spend the rest of my life giving my time, money, and skills to worthwhile endeavors where I could make a difference. I didn't know exactly what I would do, but I wanted to help save lives, solve important problems, and give more young people the chance to live their dreams" (Clinton, W. J., 2007). This sounds like the beginnings of a personal vision statement for former President Bill Clinton similar to the one you completed in Chapter 2. This statement has passion and conviction. Are you passionate about a cause?

Volunteer opportunities are available to match almost everyone's interests. There are so many worthy organizations and causes that are always in need of non-paid workers, especially those with the talent and skill base *Gap-Timers* possess. According to the U.S. Bureau of Labor Statistics (December 2002), the percentage of volunteers aged 65 and older comprise 45% of religious volunteers, 18% of the social/community services, 10% of hospital and health volunteers, 8% of civic, professional and international volunteers, 7 % of educational or youth services, 4 % in sports, hobby, cultural or arts work, and 1 % of environmental volunteers. The majority of these volunteers, 43 %, approached the organization to volunteer and 40% were approached by the organizations.

The great thing is that you can explore what you would like to do before making any kind of a commitment. If you are already volunteering somewhere that "enlivens" you, you may want to volunteer more hours. The main reasons people perform volunteer work is that it is rewarding, it maintains contact with others, it's important work, and it's often a great mental replacement for a job. Volunteer duties can keep you mentally and intellectually challenged and stimulated. Like a job, it's a matter of finding the right position for your skills, experiences and desires, such as building and repairing; working with and for different generations; helping with health care; helping the homeless; feeding the hungry; protecting the environment and animals; preserving the past; counseling, teaching, and tutoring; reducing bigotry, prejudice, and racism; and campaigning, communicating, and collecting.

Karen lived in New Jersey, and while her early years included many pleasant memories of her grandmother, she remembered the day they were walking and encountered a homeless person. Karen's first reaction was to try and help the man, but her grandmother told her that he wanted to be left alone. Karen couldn't erase the picture of that homeless man. She got married, had two sons, and got divorced. In other words, she was too busy with her own life to think about someone else's life. Feelings of "something is missing," would trouble Karen at the end of the work day. Karen's job would take her to New York where she began to notice the growing numbers of street people. That was especially true around Grand Central Station. Among them was an elderly woman. "One day, in 1981, she saw that woman sitting on a crate, and although she was late for a luncheon meeting, Karen impulsively crossed the street to a deli, bought a ham and cheese sandwich, and gave it to her. The woman touched her hand

and said, 'God bless you!' and Karen lingered to talk with her" (Kasich, J., 1998). From this experience, Karen understood that "Millie" needed the human contact just as much if not more than the sandwich. Through Karen's passion, she was instrumental in the development of the National Interfaith Hospitality Network, which has 10 churches and synagogues providing shelter and food on a rotational basis.

Perhaps you already know what skills you are willing to share with others. Thousands of individuals use previous business or job skills and their creativity to solve problems. One such example is Joanne Alter, who developed an inner-school reading program called WITS (Working In The Schools). Ms. Alter enlisted other retirees to serve as tutors in a one-on-one reading program in a school located in one of Chicago's worst neighborhoods (Freudenheim, E., 2004).

Some *Gap-Timers* will be drawn to volunteer jobs that utilize similar skills for which they were once paid. I serve on the Board of Project Performance Corporation (PPC). I enjoy the opportunity to work with PPC's president, Mike Nigro, and I love staying active in the business of business. PPC places a strong emphasis on volunteer services and good work, and it gives me great satisfaction to be associated with these wonderful people. Hopefully, they are benefitting from my years of experience and expertise.

My good friend, Jim, retired after a long career as a financial manager in the broadcasting industry. Like me, he was looking forward to slowing down vs. lying down, and wanted to put the skills he had acquired over the years to good use through volunteerism. After leaving his professional job, he found that he missed the camaraderie that his professional organization provided. He attended a chapter meeting for an organization called SCORE (*www.score*.org)—which counsels and provides real world experience to small business owners—and enjoyed the cordial, friendly atmosphere. From that meeting, he knew that SCORE was for him, and now serves on its national board. "Being able to spend time counseling and mentoring existing business owners as well as those planning a business gives me a great deal of satisfaction," says Jim. "I greatly enjoy the time I can spend with my family and friends in activities such as travel, tennis, ballroom dancing, and such. But I also enjoy the ability to offer my time in a volunteer role as my way to give back to the community."

There are many examples of folks who traded in their official hats to find themselves doing work of a very similar nature in a non-profit that fits their passion. There's the corporate attorney who is now providing pro-bono legal services for his synagogue, or the hairdresser who provides styling services to nursing homes. They are keeping their skills sharp, and reaping the rewards of helping others. They are also likely enjoying a more relaxed schedule and less day-to-day pressure.

Perhaps like Ed Boyer, you're a trail blazer. As a pilot, someone asked Ed to transport a patient with a rare disease to a specialized hospital. Then came a second and third request. After flying many patients, mostly children, he began to see a need, and in 1972 founded Mercy Medical Airlift—the nation's first medical air-transportation charity. (Treen, J. 2008). *Gap-Time* is the perfect time to explore those ideas that have been lingering around in the back of your mind. You don't have to be a celebrity to start a foundation or charitable organization. You just have to be a person with an idea and a passion to see it fulfilled.

Maybe you'll end up staying at the same organization, but in a volunteer capacity. "Ken Brown, an engineer who worked at construction oversight during the restoration of the Ellis Island National Immigration Museum in the 1970s, now works as a part-time volunteer at the same place, helping to solve maintenance-engineering problems" (Freudenheim, E., 2004).

A former editor-in-chief of *Car and Driver* discovered his volunteer path as an ambulance driver. "There should be an aspect of volunteer work that is deeply satisfying, whether it's raising a guide dog for the blind, or building houses for hurricane refugees. There should also be a challenge involved, which could be acquiring a new skill—say, learning to use a chain saw to clear brush off hiking trails—or overcoming a hesitation or fear, maybe by becoming a hospice volunteer. It's that second element, the one that demands mental or emotional growth that will keep volunteer work compelling and fresh . . . . His [Steve's] participation in the group has enriched his life. And that's the secret: finding volunteer work that works for you" (Crandell, 2007).

Others volunteer in fields that have no apparent connection with previous employment. When Don traded in the controls of a DC3 after a 34-year career with the Federal Aviation Administration, he started his "volunteer career." By volunteer career, I mean that Don works six to 10 hours each day as his church's building manager. "I needed a reason to get out of bed each morning and to focus on something other than myself. I started this volunteer job after the church was built, and have been here ever since. I know the buildings inside and out, and can save time when there is a need to locate a certain piping system in a freeze or flood situation." Using his rich work experience and natural abilities, the fixer-uppers at both the church and the school fall under Don's careful eye and attention to detail. Having someone dedicated to the facilities provides continuity in construction methods, and saves the church an actual salary or consultant fees. Don's May 2008 birthday ushers in his 90th year on this earth.

The approach to finding your volunteer niche is similar to the approach you used in your job search. Research organizations of interest to you, and find a role within the organization which fits your skill set and/or challenges you.

"While we don't all have the same amount of money, we do have access to the same 24 hours in every day" (Clinton, W. J., 2007). Volunteering isn't just busy work. It enables you to make wonderful use of your time and talents while you reap rich rewards through social interaction and a call to your "higher self."

When I was at Stanford University, I had 15 student assistants working with me in the field of counseling and psychology. I encouraged them to volunteer at our local Veterans Administration Hospital. At first, they were a little hesitant, but eventually they got their class schedules to work around their volunteer time. They would play board games with patients who had just returned from Vietnam. Many of them confided to me years later that that was one of the most rewarding experiences of their college years.

I've held many volunteer positions in my lifetime, and I've enjoyed them all immensely. I served on the Board of the Special Olympics in Louisiana—what a great organization. Likewise, I served on the Board of the American Red Cross of Baton Rouge, and we helped when major disasters occurred. You may go in with the purpose of helping others, but somehow it turns into more of a learning experience for you. When I was secretary of the Department of Environmental Quality in Louisiana, we organized "Beach Sweep," where we would get folks to come clean up our natural resources on the coast line. Through my interactions with these people who came from many different backgrounds and cultures, I learned a great deal. At the end of the day, we all joined together for a good cause, and we felt good about ourselves. I've always received more than I've given through volunteering. It's funny that you think you're giving the gift when, in fact, you turn out to be the recipient. It's a magical thing that happens. My good friend Nick often reminds me of a favorite quote, "As you climb the ladder of success, you should pause on each rung and help someone else on their way up." The true essence of volunteerism is reaching out your hand and helping others.

I hope you are feeling just a little inspired right now, and are getting a picture in your mind of what you can give back in terms of money, time, things, and skills to your community, your state, your country, or your world. It's time to focus on you and your *Gap-Time* plans for volunteering. Take some time to identify the causes that you are passionate about. Your response to volunteer work should be from a sense of "joy" and not "duty."

Think back on other volunteer activities in which you previously paticipated. Activities that proceed from fear or obligation deaden you, while activities that proceed from joy or personal intention enliven you (Cohen, A. H., 2002). If you liked serving as a volunteer before retirement, chances are strong that you will like volunteering after retirement even more. Use the information obtained in previous chapters to discover your volunteer passions. Maybe you are passionate about "going green," and want to make a difference in sustaining our natural resources. There is a great book called *Edens Lost & Found: How Ordinary Citizens are Restoring Our Great American Cities,* by Harry Wiland and Dale Bell that might give you some great ideas on how to make a difference in your community. There are so many ways to make a difference and add meaning to your life—just look at the stories in this book. Besides adding meaning and purpose to your life, there is a genuine need for your skills, talents, and time.

There are also the times that you choose to do something because someone you know asked you to do it, and you comply because you would like to make that person happy. The difference in *Gap-Time* is in knowing why you said "yes." Did you say "yes" because you wanted to serve and support your friend, or because you were afraid to say "no"? *Gap-Timers* not only find their "yes" voice, but they pursue it with passion. They also, however, find their "no" voice and use it liberally.

Now, it is your turn to identify some possible volunteer activities that match you. Please complete the following sentences by filling in your responses.

- The primary reason I don't volunteer now is: _____.
- The primary reason I do volunteer now is: _____.
- I wish I could help (people, places, or things): _____.
- If there were one cause that I identify with the most, that would be: _____.
- I know someone who volunteers as a: _____.
- Volunteering with someone that I know (would/would not) make a difference.
- I have really admired the following organization for their charity work: _____.

Now write down three possible volunteer activities that you might enjoy.

1. _____;
2. _____;
3. _____.

For each possible volunteer activity that you listed above, check (√) the motivation factors you have for each activity.

Activities	Sense of Satisfaction	Have Special Qualities or Skills	Make a Difference	Obligation to Give Back	New Skills and New Acquaintances	Something to Do
Volunteer Activity #1						
Volunteer Activity #2						
Volunteer Activity #3						

By now you should have a good idea about what kind of volunteering matches you, your personality, and skills. Know your charity and know yourself.

Volunteering can take you around the world as well. The Conservation Education Diving Awareness Marine-research (CEDAM) International is a nonprofit organization dedicated to understanding, protecting, and preserving the world's marine resources. Divers actively participate in scientific research and conservation-oriented education projects. For more information, go to *www.cedam.org*. Ever think about going on an expedition? Volunteer with Earthwatch and your time could be spent in one of 50 or so countries around the world, working on scientific field research. To learn more, go to *www.earthwatch.org*.

Have a medical background? Check out Health Volunteers Overseas and Medical Ministry International. Volunteers choose one or more weeks working in a medical, dental, surgical, or eye clinic overseas (Wagner, T. & Day, B., 1998).

If outdoors is for you, try volunteering at a campground with the National Forest Service, or serving as a Passport In Time (PIT) volunteer, also with the U.S. Forest Service (Kerschner, H. K. & Hansan, J. E. (Eds.)., 1996).

If you need some help identifying organizations, get ready. Generically, there are community institutions, such as churches, synagogues, political parties, hospitals, art societies, and museums. To start, look in your own backyard—think locally. Research charitable organizations in your town or city. There is likely a volunteer job bank which posts open positions. If you don't see one that fits your skill set and/or interests, make an appointment with someone on staff to help guide you to the appropriate organization. For very specific recommendations, you could try the AARP's Volunteer Talent Bank and Points of Light Foundation (that has recently joined with Hands On Network). The website for the Volunteer Talent Bank is: *www.seniors-site.com/retiremt/aarp.html*. The websites for Points of Light Foundation and Hands On are: *www.pointsoflight.org/* and *www.handsonnetwork.org*, respectively.

In no particular order, here are some other worthy causes:

Help abused men/women/children;
Work with troubled teens;
Walk people's dogs or baby-sit other pets;
Baby-sit grandchildren, neighbors' children;
Read to and/or visit bedridden people;
Study/teach Braille;
Help/visit someone taking chemotherapy;
Improve the environment;
Assist handicapped people;
Use your legal knowledge to help immigrants or refugees to the United States;
Visit nursing homes;
Help someone with Parkinson's disease;
Build a park;
Work a suicide hot line;
Teach someone a foreign language;

Counsel young people on life decisions;
Volunteer at a school;
Teach sign language; or
Use your fundraising skills for community improvements;

Volunteering can be an incredibly rewarding experience in your *Gap-Time*. You may find a renewed sense of purpose and/or learn a whole new skill set. Volunteering is also an awesome way to build your social network as previously discussed in Chapter 5. You will already have a common interest with the folks you meet while volunteering so there's a good likelihood that some new friendships will result from those you meet.

Happy volunteering!

> That is happiness; to be dissolved into something that is complete and great.
>
> Willa Cather (The Little Zen Companion)

Chapter 8

All Gap-Timers want to do is have some fun!

"You will do foolish things, but do them with enthusiasm."
—Colette

"When I visited the Soviet Union with Dr. Patch Adams, he wore his outlandish clown outfit nearly everywhere and distributed red rubber noses all over Russia. One day, Patch approached a very serious-looking army officer guarding Red Square, and put a rubber nose on him. I thought for sure he was going to start a war! But after a few moments, the guard smiled and broke into a laugh. Even more than being a tough guy, the soldier wanted to laugh" (Cohen, A. H., 2002). You have to define your own fun.

Adventure combined with youth can be exhilarating, but adventure combined with age can also be exhilarating. When just out of college, I took my American Express card and headed off to Europe. My first purchase was the book, *Europe on $5 a Day*. I spent several glorious months traveling around—what a fabulous experience. Ahh, youth. When I look back, however, on my tracks, trails, and traverses (title of my next book, by the way, so stay tuned!), I see where my journey has taken me. I've been to Ireland; Paris; London; Johannesburg, South Africa; Soviet Union; Romania; Mexico; Puerto Rico; Greece; the Middle East; Japan, Taiwan Hong Kong, Vietnam; Northern Africa; Reykjavik, Iceland; West Indies; and many more. You name it, I've been there, and plan to go again! People often ask me how many languages I speak. I understand some French, but a smile can get you anywhere.

Like to travel? Want to be paid while you travel? There is at least one book on working your way around the world when you retire (Griffith, S., 2005). There are several international placement organizations that are accustomed to assisting students, and are now helping adults secure employment abroad. If you don't happen to secure employment before arriving, then the recommendation is to network along the way with fellow travelers. Another recommendation is to apply for casual work in more rural or rustic areas. Showing up around holidays is usually a pretty good method for getting immediate employment, too. Seasonal sports activities spur temporary employment.

Working for cruise liners is also a fascinating way to see different seas and lands. Beware, however, of agents promising high-paying jobs and short hours. There are a number of websites available to you for conducting your own research. Private yacht owners will hire on crew between ports of call or for an entire cruise. If you lack sea legs, overland tours may be for you. If you take the time to earn special driving or other licenses, you could find yourself in high demand. The methodology is to travel to your starting point with a plan and some money. You save money while you work so you can travel to the next town or the next country.

Traveling by train is not something that Americans do with any frequency, but it certainly is done extensively in Europe. What about working for the rail line? In addition to getting paid, some employers provide free travel to their employees on their days off. I have a very good friend, Gaynor, who plays the piano. Six months out of the year, she travels by train across country, playing the piano in the club car. When she is not on the train, she is on a ship, the *Sea Cloud*, playing for packed rooms. There is no limit to where you can go. Gaynor is delighted to be able to show off her talents, entertaining folks and seeing the countryside all at the same time. Gaynor isn't doing anything that you can't do with a little thought and creativity. As you discovered in Chapter 7, there are plenty of volunteer opportunities that can provide enormous opportunities for fun and adventure. Don't let your age limit you. Focus on what you have to offer, not your limitations. Let your desire for fun and adventure be your guide.

There are thousands and thousands of amazing stories of seniors achieving what their idea of fun is. "Norman Vaughan, 99, the last surviving member of Admiral Byrd's 1925 Antarctic expedition, who is planning a 100th birthday party atop Mt. Vaughn, the forbidding 10,000-foot Antarctic peak named after him" (Hansen, M. V. & Linkletter, A., 2006). Other stories include a 71-year-old who, in 2005, completed a horseback ride to all 48 state capitals in the continental United States to raise money for the children of Paraguay; an 80-year-old who, in 2004, completed a bicycle ride from San Diego, California to Jacksonville Beach, Florida to raise money and national awareness for the homeless; a 91-year—old who, in 2004, won the Women's 10 slalom and tricks event at the Annual Water Ski National Championships; a 64-year-old former homeless man who's now one of the best softball players in the country; and a 105-year-old co-founder of the San Francisco Art Students League and the Oak Group in Santa Barbara, still a very active California landscape artist (Hansen, M. V. & Linkletter, A., 2006).

There are so many more stories to share, and each of them is more remarkable than the one before. My idea of fun is to buy myself a shrimp boat and hire a captain to run it. Every Friday, I'd have him send me 50 pounds of fresh shrimp for the weekly party I'd host for all my friends. Now that might not seem like fun to you, but it's been a dream of mine for a long time, and hopefully one day, I'll discover how much fun it really is. My friends think I'm crazy. "Martha," they tell me, "that would be a horrible investment." They don't see my vision, but that's okay. It's my *Gap-Time* and not theirs. It's my fun; they need to catch up! I may even take them for a ride one day on my shrimp boat, and I bet they will help me eat some shrimp!

While I'm waiting to buy my shrimp boat, I find it fun to see movies and spend time with friends. Since I entered my *Gap-Time*, I've had more time to re-connect with dear pals from my past. My first-grade friend, Bess, and I started writing more. It's wonderful to reminisce with her about the good old days—baking cookies at my house, chatting about teachers we both had, etc. My *Gap-Time* also allows me opportunities to pursue my love of festivals and attending spectator sports. I love the energy you can only find at a packed stadium or arena.

I used to salivate when people talked about a book they were reading, and I'd think with envy about the stack of biographies and non-fiction volumes waiting for me on my nightstand. I used to really enjoy competing in chili cook-offs around the globe. Crawfish chili is my specialty and I am the creator. I've mixed my magic in Texas, Louisiana, Mexico, Guadalajara, and other various locales where folks want to taste and compare chili.

Believe it or not, I haven't found any time for my chili passion in my *Gap-Time*, but I do enjoy cooking. I also occasionally indulge my guilty pleasure of watching game shows—hey, it's educational! The *Price is Right* tests my supermarket knowledge of current prices. I like to consider it 30 minutes of my continuing education.

The idea is to turn your downtime into fun and/or relaxing time. If you're anything like me, your career probably didn't allow for much downtime. When I finally found myself with some extra time on my hands, I didn't quite know what to do with myself. I felt anxious. I always felt like I needed to be doing something. *Must be productive. Must be accomplishing. Must keep the wheels turning.* I had to learn how to relax. Whew. What a wonderful lesson it turned out to be. Now, I look forward to enjoying quiet time, and I've learned that quiet time can be fun. I pick up one of the books on my nightstand and/or spend an evening with Pat Sajak and Vanna White, and marvel at my ability to put those phrases together! We previously discussed things to do when you're by yourself, so maybe this is a good time to go back and review that information. Cherish your downtime. Use it to refuel and get ready for your next grand adventure.

I've added some of my favorite "fun" activities along with those generated by Tricia Wagner and Barbara Day in their book, *How to Enjoy Your Retirement*. In no particular order, here is a long list of some fun activities to meet all interests:

Visit a toy store and buy the first thing that catches your eye;
Visit a museum;
Walk around a pet store;
Indulge in your favorite magazine and head to a coffee shop you've never been to before—make it a mission to check out a new one every week;

Go to an art store. Buy a few art supplies and paint or sketch something;
Learn to play a musical instrument(s);
Join a band and/or have a "jam session" with other musicians;
Collect/build/fly model airplanes;
Learn about gardening/insects/diseases;
Buy/sell items at an auction or on E-bay;
Unclutter your house and host a yard sale;
Get tickets to your favorite talk show and become a member of the audience;
Learn about the different qualities of gems and crystals;
Make jewelry;
Learn to read tarot cards;
Learn to cook/bake;
Join a singing group;
Study/visit famous cathedrals/basilicas;
Walk/vacation on the beach;
Join a book club;
Take up hiking and discover the trails near where you live;
Bicycle for fun and exercise;
Learn and follow the stock market;
Make/buy fine wood furniture;
Study/practice calligraphy;
Volunteer for a political campaign;
Learn to draw cartoons;
Go to a paint-your-own-pottery place;
Learn to play chess and enter tournaments;
Research your family tree;
Collect/buy/sell/trade comic books;
Go cross-country skiing;
Take a cruise. Once onboard, enter the costume contest;
Pick a room in your house and re-design it;

Take a defensive driving course;
Make plans to visit a dude ranch;
Join a sports league;
Watch/study/travel to see the next eclipse;
Buy a telescope and learn about the constellation;
Attend/enter a state/county fair and/or chili cook-off;
Write a poem/song/novel/fairy tale;
Build a patio/walkway/fountain/barbecue;
Research the history and culture of your favorite country;
Hunt game birds;
Play golf/tennis and enter tournaments;
Become a gourmet cook;
Learn about wines;
Visit all 5 Great Lakes;
Enjoy a trip to Hawaii, the Caribbean, or Mexican ports of call;
Take a helicopter flight;
Take flying lessons;
Study/grow/use herbs;
Raise honeybees and sell their honey;
Figure out a way to turn your favorite hobby into a business;
Keep a journal;
Learn to juggle;
Learn to kayak;
Audition for a role in a play at your community theater;
Write articles for your local paper;
Make a scrapbook for someone you love;
Take a photography class and enter a photo contest;
Learn a new language;
Pick an author and read everything he/she has ever written;
Read a classic;
Make it a point to see every movie that is nominated for an Oscar;

Learn how to decorate cakes;
Speak publicly about your favorite researched subject;
Visit a nursing home;
Monitor the state legislature;
Build model rockets;
Learn how to fly fish and make your own fishing lures;
Perform magic tricks;
Become a ham radio operator;
Pack up a picnic and head to the great outdoors;
Serve as a master of ceremony for a function;
Run for mayor/legislator/governor/president;
Practice something every day to improve your memory;
Learn/teach sign language;
Start a coin/stamp collection;
Participate in a medieval fair in costume;
Host a themed costume party;
Take your dog to obedience school;
Buy a surplus of cards and pick a person to send one to each week;
Go see a Broadway show;
Plant a tree;
Pick wild flowers and put them in a vase;
Learn to arrange flowers;
Grow flowers from seeds;
Play with/swim with the dolphins;
Wallpaper a room;
Design/build/ride on a parade float (it's Mardi Gras time!);
Learn to make homemade pasta and then invite some friends over to eat it;
Buy/show/raise purebred dogs/cats/horses;
Make your own holiday decorations;
Build a playhouse for kids;
Read/write/publish poetry;

Play cards;
Start a bridge club;
Work puzzles/Sudoku/crossword puzzles;
Collect/trade/sell model trains;
Become a skilled storyteller;
Referee sporting events;
Take classes at the universities, community colleges, health care facilities, YMCAs/YWCAs;
Register to take a retreat;
Enjoy a spa day;
Learn to sail and join a club;
Collect/build model ships;
Learn to scuba dive;
Learn to skydive;
Try snow/water skiing;
Try snow boarding;
Sing/write a song;
Travel where you've always wanted to go;
Set up/maintain an aquarium;
Learn to re-upholster furniture;
Usher at your place of worship;
Improve your vocabulary;
Repair watches;
Build clocks;
Study/record/report weather conditions;
Take a ride on a shrimp boat;
Take a water safety class;
Learn CPR;
Practice yoga;
Design your own personal stationery;
Make copies of your favorite pictures and pass along to family and friends;

Plan an adventure in your own city—check out the public transportation system;
Go somewhere you've never been and talk to "strangers" who may be your neighbors;
Sing karaoke;
Write a story about your childhood and give it to your grandchild;
Buy a new pair of walking shoes and use them;
Get your palm read;
Host a dinner party;
Check out an organic market or your local farmer's market;
Go antiquing;
Make a reservation at a new restaurant in your neighborhood;
Learn to play poker;
Research your sun sign;
Buy a joke book and memorize a few good ones;
Learn how to make soap or candles and give them as gifts[1];
Get a massage;
Give a massage;
Clean out your closets and donate unwanted, gently used items to charity;
Learn to knit; or
Educate yourself on how to "go green" and reduce your energy costs.
*(Wagner, T. & Day, B., 1998). (*Inspired by)

[1] In the 1970s, I designed and had a retired dentist help me make candles bearing the crest of my sorority, Zeta Tau Alpha. (I got a patent on it). I formed a mail order business and sold them all over the United States. It only takes one idea and some courage to put it into action.

The bottom line is that your idea of fun and my idea of fun are probably vastly different. Find your own fun and follow it wherever it leads you. If you're still in a fun rut, hopefully, the list above and the other information presented in this Chapter has helped you identify some playful activities you'd like to explore and some creative ways to spend your downtime. Create your very own fun list and save it for a rainy day. The idea is to be active, stay active, play, and have fun. I have friends who are acting "old" in their retirement. They sit around and talk about their past careers, the price of gas, and what their neighbors are doing. I don't mean to brag, but they are aging much quicker than I am! Truth be told, I think they're a little boring, but don't tell them I told you!

Life is what we make it, therefore we should work earnestly and look hopefully into the future. Destiny has flung her misty curtain across the path of every mortal's life, and until that path be trodden, no one knows the secrets of that vague domain.

—Mammy Fletcher

Chapter 9

One size does not fit all

"No amount of skillful invention can replace the essential element of imagination."

—Edward Hopper

There is room for everyone and their individual *Gap-Time* plans. Comparing yourself and what you want for your life to others and what they want for their lives is destructive behavior. In 1952, Max Ehrmann wrote *Desiderata*. "If you compare yourself with others, you may become vain and bitter; for always there will be greater and lesser persons than yourself. Enjoy your achievements as well as your plans."

Accepting your worth and wholeness will free you from regarding someone else as superior.

Being your authentic self and embracing your uniqueness and creativity does not take away from others; it empowers them. Consequently, whatever you envision for your life will not work for others. Trials and tribulations are part of the journey; however, almost every difficult situation can be an opportunity. Remember that every difficult situation eventually becomes a badge that you will probably wear proudly (Keoghan, P., 2004).

Practice the butterfly principles. "When you begin a new project, when you want to make a dream come true, when you begin a new phase in any way, prepare yourself mentally, . . ." (Kustenmacher, T., 2004). Use the active voice when writing your goals and be very specific about the results you want to see. Feel your wings. "Have faith that there are undiscovered capabilities lying dormant within you—your butterfly wings—which you can develop and use. The essentials do not come to you from outside; they reside within you and they just need to be awakened" (Kustenmacher, T., 2004).

To punctuate each person's uniqueness, there is a company called Vocation Vacations based in Portland, Oregon (*www.vocationvacations.com*) that allows you to try out certain kinds of jobs during your vacation (Keoghan, P., 2004). What about inventing something? Are you handy with tools or creating unusual recipes in the kitchen? Not everyone has both the skills and the "desire" to pursue the same hobbies or interests.

Let's take a few minutes to identify some areas that you are likely to differ from others in their *Gap-Time* plan.

- What I want out of life;
- What I want from retirement;
- What role work will play in my future;

- What jobs (if I work) provide me with the rewards that I seek;
- What challenges I enjoy most;
- What the most meaningful experiences in my life are;
- What stress/pressure in my life am I willing to tolerate;
- What dreams I have.

You will not find anyone who has the same parts as you do for your *Gap-Time* plan. "Many people of this generation are catching the vision in giving their life away as a route to true fulfillment.... The people making this transition to service have come to their decision after wrestling with the idea that there must be more to life. Those who have pursued religious studies later in life share two essential traits: (1) they were willing to risk, and (2) they were willing to search" (Anthony, M., 2001).

The set of exercises that follow will help you to identify what's unique about you. Are you willing to search? In the following table, list 15 to 20 achievements. You could probably list hundreds! Some examples are: started a small paper route and built it up with new customers; learned to play the piano and often played for my church; created, and assembled an award-winning science fair project; helped develop the first website for my high school; first in my family to attend college; received my Master's degree; awarded a full academic scholarship; awarded outstanding citizenship award in my community; organized fundraiser for church; etc. (Krannich, R. & Krannich, C., 2005).

Achievement Statements	Place a check mark (√) by your top seven achievements	How did I initially become involved?	What did I do?
#1			
#2			
#3			
#4			
#5			
#6			
#7			
#8			
#9			
#10			
#11			
#12			
#13			
#14			
#15			
#16			
#17			
#18			
#19			
#20			

Let's understand your emotions and commitment for three of your top achievement statements. Fill in the information in the following table.

Achievement Statements	What was involved in the achievement?	What was your part?	What did you actually do?	How did you go about that?
Achievement Statement #1				
Achievement Statement #2				
Achievement Statement #3				

Identify the recurring skills, abilities, and personal qualities demonstrated in your achievements:

Your *Gap-Time* plan is your burning desire that drives your dedicated action. "Every second of your life contains the raw ingredients you need to seize an opportunity that will make your life more rewarding" (Dorsey, J. R., 2007). We each have a unique thumbprint. As a counselor of young people for many, many years, the fundamental principle that I lived by was that there was no cookie-cutter process or system for how I could counsel the kids in my charge. Each and every one of them was different. They each had their own talents, issues, skills, sensitivities, etc. I couldn't assume that just because I was talking to a 15-year-old Hispanic girl that she was going to have similar responses or reactions to any of the other 15-year-old Hispanic girls I happened to be counseling. That would have been a huge mistake. In an academic setting, it is sometimes difficult to see that uniqueness because there are rules and regulations that everyone is expected to follow. As individuals, it is how we develop and integrate ourselves into society and how we imprint our thumbprints out in the world that really matters.

With time and a little creativity, you'll create your own *Gap-Time* thumbprint. Remember—no two are alike. My dreams for my *Gap-Time* will be different from yours. Yours will be different from your friends, relatives, and co-workers. Think back to the differences discussed earlier, i.e., "old" retirement vs. "new" retirement. Reflect on what your parents', or even your grandparents', retirement looked like. Note the differences.

"My parents are from an environment where the government, banks, and institutions cannot be trusted," says Dong. "Their experience is not so much the rule of law that we have in this country, but the rule of self-reliance. In a sense, they never retire. They must always seek to ensure that they have the means to sustain themselves. This is true even though they have made enough for themselves to stop working. That sense of insecurity will never leave them. On the other hand, although my face and my name is Korean, it is the American education and culture that allows me to relax in comparison to my parents. I see and understand the system. I see the strengths and weaknesses of this country. We are blessed with the rule of law, our voice in determining the course of our affairs, and institutions that work. I think of retirement as a 'promotion,' and I think of how I can work to achieve that goal. And, I have a sense of security that is absent in my parents because I am a product of this culture." As you envision your parents' and grandparents' retirements, think about the options you have that weren't available to them.

Be a trailblazer and follow your own dreams. Back in 1993, I bought a track of land in Louisiana and developed it into a subdivision now called Madden Cove. There are 14 lots, all of which face the lake on Toledo Bend. At the time, all my friends thought I was crazy. My vision, however, was to someday build my own place. Way back then, I had a *Gap-Time* vision, and I stuck to it even though I wasn't getting much support. My good friend, Barney, helped and guided me on many of the steps in this development. He was invaluable. I had to build a 9/10 of a mile road to access it. If you want to spend lots of money, this is the quickest way. I stuck it out, and needless to say, that vision turned out to be a pretty good investment. My friends aren't thinking I'm so crazy now. In fact, some have bought lots on Madden Cove.

It is important to discuss your *Gap-Time* vision with your loved ones and get their buy-in and support. While I was able to ignore the pleadings of friends, it's probably not a good idea to move forward with a major decision without the support of your spouse or partner. Your wife may have a vision of traveling and seeing the world once your hectic careers are behind you. You, on the other hand, may envision a life of relaxation which involves little more than toting your fishing pole and some bait down to the lake behind your house—which you could do if you lived on Madden Cove. Communication and compromise are key to making sure that your relationships stay intact throughout your *Gap-Time*. Again—a plan without flexibility is nothing more than a fantasy. Listen to your partner and incorporate their vision into yours.

Man's main task in life is to give birth to himself.

Erich Fromm (The Little Zen Companion)

Chapter 10

Are you stuck?

> "One does not discover new lands without consenting to lose sight of the shore for a very long time."
> —André Gide

If you are uninspired in the real world and can't identify what most brings meaning and/or happiness and joy to your life, you're stuck. Peeling away the illusions that have you stuck reveals your genius, your uniqueness, and your creativity. "Some people discover their passion only to feel so overwhelmed by all the work it will take to realize it that they procrastinate" (Dorsey, J. R., 2007). "Concentrate on the beginning. If your mind knows that you are managing to do what you have taken on, you can let go of the goal while you are doing the task. That will seem strange to goal-oriented people. But concentrate on the beginning—the first step. Get absorbed in the doing instead of becoming obsessed with the end-result. Develop a love of the journey—not just the destination" (Kustenmacher, T., 2004).

Signs You May Be Stuck:

- You're spending more than one hour a day in front of the TV.
- You've invited your crazy, unemployed cousin Edith to move in for an undetermined amount of time.
- Your entire day is spent doing other people's errands, tasks, etc.
- You answer "no" when asked, "Can I be myself?"
- You answer "no" when asked, "Can I say what I feel?"
- You answer "no" when asked, "Can I be loved?"
- You are afraid that you are inferior.
- You are afraid that you are vulnerable.
- You are afraid that you deserve to be rejected.

The best way to figure out what to do may be to just get quiet and let your inner voice provide some much needed guidance. Let's start with something simple. Write short answers to the right of each question. Notice there are open parentheses at the beginning of each question. Instructions will be given at the completion. Some of these questions come from Jason Ryan Dorsey's book, *My Reality Check Bounced!* (Dorsey, J. R., 2007.)

( ) What shoes will you wear to work?
( ) What shoes will you wear if you are not working?
( ) What will your workplace sound like at 3:00 PM?
( ) What will your schedule be at 3:00 PM if you are not working?
( ) What will be your main responsibility?
( ) Who will you talk most with on the phone?
( ) What will be the view from your front door?

( ) What will be the view from your back door?
( ) What relationships will you cherish the most?
( ) What will your friends and family say to strangers about you?
( ) How will you physically feel when you wake up?
( ) How will you relax each day?
( ) What do you spend the most time doing Monday through Friday?
( ) What do you spend the most time doing on Saturdays?
( ) What do you spend the most time doing on Sundays?
( ) What makes you feel most alive?
( ) What is the greatest memory you will have?
( ) How will you contribute time, money, and energy to your community?
( ) What will be your biggest legacy to the world?
( ) What will people say at your funeral?

Now, go back through the list of questions and make a check mark (√) by the five questions that caused you the most discomfort in responding to, or that you didn't answer at all.

Now, let's move those five questions into the following table to identify contributors to your feelings. Make a check mark (√) in the column(s) that identify those contributors.

Questions	Specific Behaviors of Others	My Behaviors	Equally My Behaviors and Those of Others
#1			
#2			
#3			
#4			
#5			

Do you see a pattern of behavior either in yourself or others that contributes to your feelings? With the information that you gleaned from your responses above, can you see whether or not part of being stuck can be attributed to others and partly to you?

Now, let's do a quick review of the obstacles you wrote down that would keep you from achieving your vision (Chapter 2). Write those obstacles in the following table and then check (√) the column that is appropriate if the major obstacle is with others or with you, or shared equally by you and others.

Obstacle	Specific Behaviors of Others	My Behaviors	Equally My Behaviors and Those of Others

You should start to see a clear pattern of behavior either in yourself or others that contribute to your feelings.

Unearthing and trusting your creativity may be a new behavior for you. You may feel and act erratic. This is all part of getting unstuck—pulling free from the attitudes, beliefs, people, places, and things that have "blocked" you in the past.

Per Claudia Black, "Surround yourself with people who respect and treat you well." This is a great piece of advice anytime, but especially in your *Gap-Time*. Do not expect your friends who are also "stuck" to applaud your efforts to get unstuck. Getting "unstuck" raises the unsettling possibility that they, too, could become "unstuck" and move into authentic creative risks rather than bench-sitting cynicism (Cameron, J., 1992). These friends may feel abandoned and could unconsciously try to guilt-trip you into giving up your new, healthy habits. In addition to folks who may try to sabotage your recovery beyond "stuck," there are others in your life who enjoy wreaking havoc. Julia Cameron refers to these individuals as "crazymakers" (Cameron, J., 1992).

"Crazymakers are those personalities that create storm centers. They are charismatic, highly inventive and powerfully persuasive." Crazymakers will do their best to upset your plans; they are "enormously destructive . . . long on problems and short on solutions." They are slick, sly creatures who feed on drama. They are so slick, in fact, that you may not even realize that their drama is spilling over into your plans. Or maybe you do. Cameron asserts that we intentionally put those crazymakers in our own path as a distraction to our own goals. Hmm. Crazymakers come in various packages of "fixer-uppers." Some are irresistible and pull you in the direction of intervention on their behalf to make changes in them. However, crazymakers are not interested in recovering from their role. They like drama, as they have center-stage attention, and they spend a great deal of energy maintaining that position.

I've always been a rather ambitious self-starter of things which a number of people aren't always that supportive of in the professional arena. Productive people draw attention to non-productive people. At times, the non-productive people would not be supportive of my efforts and/or projects. I didn't let them break my spirit or distract me from my goals. If you have people like this in your life, learn to ignore their sighs and eye rolling. If your gut is telling you to buy a track of land, go for it. Listen to words of counsel and make your own decision.

"Crazymakers break deals and destroy schedules .... expect special treatment .... discount your reality .... spend your time and money .... triangulate those they deal with .... are expert blamers .... create dramas .... hate schedules .... hate order .... deny that they are crazymakers" (Cameron, J., 1992). Who are the crazymakers in your life?

Crazymaker	Wreaks Havoc by ...	I Allow This Drama in my Life Because ...	His/Her Power Would be Lessened if I ...

Perhaps you have unknowingly invited some crazymakers to set up house in your *Gap-Time*. It's a good distraction, but sooner or later you're going to have to clean house.

What are some personal reasons that could have you stuck? How many of the following descriptors fit you?

- Predictable and comfortable;
- Trapped in routines;

- Absorbed by burdens of daily life;
- Not enough money in the bank;
- Exhausting work schedule;
- Caretaking of children, adult children, or parents;
- Physically out of shape.

What are your top three responses? Is it something that you have control over?

You can only change those areas that you exercise control over. Let's work through the areas that you exercise control over and identify at least three ways you can make changes. Share the results of this exercise with a trusted friend or family member.

Personal Areas	Change #1	Change #2	Change #3
Predictable and comfortable			
Example:	Take a personal enrichment class.	Plan a dinner party in the middle of the week.	Buy and wear that red and purple hat.
Trapped in routines			
Example:	Eat eggs for breakfast instead of cereal.	Wear jeans one day a week.	Try contacts instead of glasses.
Absorbed by burdens of daily life			
Example:	Attend church services regularly.	Go to a counselor.	Absorb yourself in a fun hobby.
Not enough money in the bank;			
Example:	Get a job or a second job.	Clip coupons.	Start a home business.
Exhausting work schedule			
Example:	Change working hours.	Work part-time.	Work from home.
Care taking of children, adult children, or parents			

Example:	Hire a sitter to stay with Dad on Tuesday evenings.	Arrange for regular daycare for child or parent.	Have sibling take care of parents for two or more weeks.
I'm out of shape			
Example:	Start a walking regime.	Prepare a garden by yourself instead of hiring someone.	Join a fitness club.

In the growth process, there are steps forward, but it is also normal to experience and encounter steps that move you backward. Insights and inroads could be followed by disappointing setbacks. Perhaps you could benefit from a retirement coach. I am accredited as both a certified retirement coach and a career counselor. (For more info, check out my website at *www.gap-time.com*). I support others in their quest to find their true path; likewise, I seek the counsel of others in areas where I need support, whether it's a personal trainer or a stylist. Sometimes we turn to these people not because we're not knowledgeable, but because we need a little jumpstart or a second pair of eyes to help us see through the forest. Whatever the case, it's not an admission of failure to seek help; it's an intelligent way to fast forward through the muck and sidestep some potentially costly—financially, emotionally and otherwise—mistakes. Maybe this person is a spiritual leader vs. a coach. Whatever the case, know that there are people and resources available to you to help navigate the rough terrain on your course.

According to scientist, doctor, educator, and mother, Elisabeth Kübler-Ross, "Learn to get in touch with the silence within yourself and know that everything in this life has a purpose." (www.quotationspage.com) From your silence, embrace your optimism and prepare for adventure and surprise. Get involved and stay involved in "you" and make sure you keep dreaming. Figure out what is keeping you from those dreams. The best way to figure out what to do may be to get quiet and let your inner voice provide some much-needed guidance. Being stuck is a normal part of the process. Remaining stuck is not.

Professional retirement coaches can draw forth the best in you rather than continually directing your attention to what is wrong with you. If you are handing over your future to someone who adds to your feeling of being "stuck" and confused, instead of giving you the tools to feel lighter, freer, and stronger, it's time to walk out. A good retirement coach is authentic and walks their talk. A good coach lives a life that reflects the values they express and suggest for you. They acknowledge that they, too, are on the *Gap-Time* journey. A good retirement coach engenders a sense of shared learning and stimulates your sense that you are on a similar path. A good coach assists you to connect with your inner wisdom to get beyond "stuck," instead of forcing you to follow their direction. They respect your mind, emotions, body, and spirit, and support you to nourish all these aspects.

> How can you get very far,
> If you don't know Who You Are?
> How can you do what you ought,
> If you don't know What You've Got?
> And if you don't know Which to Do
> Of all the things in front of you,
> Then what you'll have when you are through
> Is just a mess without a clue
> Of all the best that can come true
> If you know What and Which and Who.
> *Winnie the Pooh—The Tao of Pooh*

It is good to have an end to journey toward; but it is the journey that matters, in the end.

Ursula K. Le Guin (The Little Zen Companion).

Chapter 11

Be open to the unexpected

"Trust that still, small voice that says, this might work and I'll try it."

—Diane Mariechild

As logical, rational adults, we know that we need to plan for things in life. As mature adults, we also know that the best-laid plans . . . well, you know . . . they go up in smoke. I encourage all *Gap-Timers* to plan for their retirement, but I also urge you to be open to life and expect the unexpected. I can't begin to tell you the number of times in my life that I thought I was headed in one direction and for some reason or another—a call from a boss, an unexpected job offer, etc.—my path took a turn. Something unexpected can happen when you decide to pop into a convention center to check out an exhibit or attend a new networking event. Or, like my friend, Dianne, when you change your plans to accommodate a rainy day and then find yourself opening a whole new business and becoming an artist! Some call it serendipity or accidental fortune. Others call it synchronicity or just plain ol' being in the right place at the right time. Renowned psychiatrist Carl Jung coined the word "synchronicity" to describe what he called "temporally coincident occurrences of acausal events" (*Wikipedia.org*).

"Despite all the talk about planning one's career and pursuing a passion, most people fall into jobs and careers by accident or happenstance: a part-time job that became permanent; a college research project that led to important job contacts; a casual conversation with a friend that turned into a job interview and offer; a life-changing vacation that led to important job contacts; a life-changing vacation that led to a career change; a chance meeting with a recruiter; an enthralling hobby that became a job" (Krannich, R & Krannich, C, 2005).

Whatever "it" is, it won't work if you're not open to picking up the signals the universe is sending you. You could be toying with the idea of singing on a cruise ship, and by luck (or serendipity) find yourself seated next to a ship's captain at your granddaughter's recital, who just happens to know that there's an opening for a singer in his cruise line. In order to receive your gift from the universe, you have to be paying attention, and you have to be ready to take action. This is not a time for head scratching followed by an internal, "gee, that was interesting." This is a time for conversation and vocalizing your needs and desires. Through the process of keeping a journal (as previously recommended), more and more of those buried desires will come up, and hopefully, you will be more in tune with the messages you're receiving from your subconscious and the universe.

If I haven't convinced you of the power of synchronicity, perhaps my friend Alta will. Alta spent close to 40 years in the field of education for the state of Louisiana before she retired. Alta has never *not* wanted to work and knew she would continue to do something, but she had no real idea what she wanted to do. She did, however, know two things: 1) She didn't want to continue what she had been doing; and 2) She wanted to do something entirely different from what she had been doing. She also knew that she wanted to end her professional career on a high-note. "When you are on a roll, don't wait for the rug to be pulled out from under you," warns Alta. "I retired when the wave was high."

Alta had been widowed for many years and happened to be on one of her trips to visit her daughter in Georgia when she met a man who would eventually become her husband. This man just happened to be visiting his son who lived across the street from Alta's daughter—so figure the odds. So out of the blue she meets this man, they get married, and she moves to a different state. This new life has her doing all sorts of things she never expected or planned. She got involved with her husband's car business and carried her bureaucratic knowledge over into that industry. She even sold me a car and delivered it to me in Washington, D.C. from Athens, Georgia Then she jumped in and helped him with his land development business.

"I would ride around in this truck with him looking at subdivisions," says Alta. "Then I started taking classes to become certified on land issues, and boy, I was just having a ball. I was learning new things about industries I never had a clue about. I'd be out on construction sites with my tape measure, digging around in the dirt. I would even ride in the dump trucks when they were hauling—it was just amazing to me." Alta and her husband recently celebrated their 10th wedding anniversary, and she's still saying, "I will never retire." As a matter of fact, she's teaching again. If you had the pleasure of talking to Alta, you'd be able to hear the joy in her voice. Alta found that joy because she was open to doing new things and meeting new people. She was ready for an adventure, and she got it! Would she have found that adventure and/or her husband if she had had her head buried in the sand? I'm always excited to hear what's on her plate because you just know it's not going to be dull.

In *The Artist's Way*, Julia Cameron frequently refers to the power of synchronicity. "We call it coincidence. We call it luck. We call it anything but what it is—the hand of God, or good activated by our own hand when we act in behalf of our truest dreams, when we commit to our own soul . . . As each idea comes to us, we must in good faith clear away our inner barriers to acting on it and then, on an outer level, take the concrete steps necessary to trigger our synchronous good" (Cameron, J. 1992). It would be easy for me as Dianne and Alta's friend to say, "gee, they sure are lucky," but I know better. They are women who are open to life's adventures and are ready to take action when adventure comes knocking. We can look back in history and literature to find great examples of folks who were open to all that life had to offer, but we probably won't find any greater examples than Winnie-the-Pooh.

As a matter of fact, Benjamin Hoff wrote *The Tao of Pooh*, using Pooh as an example of the wisdom of the Zen masters. Pooh approaches every day with a simple joy, with no greater goal than being with his friends in the forest and eating honey. Somehow, Pooh and his friends manage to find themselves involved in all sorts of adventures and faced with serious challenges. Yet, it is Pooh, through his natural curiosity and innocence, who seems to hold the key that solves all their problems. Says Piglet, "Pooh hasn't much Brain, but he never comes to any harm. He does silly things and they turn out right." Pooh is open to the unexpected because he doesn't know not to be open to it. He enjoys the state of the "Uncarved Block... From the state of the Uncarved Block comes the ability to enjoy the simple and the quiet, the natural and the plain. Along with that comes the ability to do things spontaneously and have them work, odd as they may appear to others at times" (Hoff, 1982).

According to the bestselling author, Marianne Williamson, "Synchronicity is the handwriting of God." If we are swimming with the tide, we will meet the people we're supposed to meet at the time we're supposed to meet them." We'll get rained in on the day we're meant to discover the paint-your-own-pottery place. If we're swimming against the tide, when the rain comes, we'll fight our inner desire to go exploring in spite of the rain. We'll likely stay inside and curse the rain while watching TV. Like everything else, the first step lies with you. It is your action or inaction that determines your destiny. I don't know of anyone who got their perfect job or met their soul mate while sitting at home on the couch. Much to our chagrin, Ed McMahon doesn't knock on many of our doors to present us with that Sweepstakes check, catching us unexpectedly, still in our bathrobe. By the way, Ed McMahon isn't the only one who has been on the *Tonight Show* with Johnny Carson. Yours truly appeared via telephone along with Johnny on millions of TV screens. You never know where your journey will take you.

In order to expect and be ready for the unexpected, you truly have to be living in the moment. So many of us are caught up in regrets of the past, resentments of yesterday's spilled milk, and worries about tomorrow's perceived challenges and disappointments, that we miss what is going on right in front of us—right now, right this instance. How many opportunities have you missed because you weren't paying attention? Or better yet—how many accidents have you had because your mind was elsewhere instead of where it should have been—looking out your rearview mirror?

A word of caution—be sure to bring your positive attitude into the present moment. I can pretty much guarantee you that the miracle of the unexpected isn't going to come exploding into your life when you're carrying around thoughts like, "I'm never going to meet any new friends," or "My life is over—I'm of no use to anyone or anything." If your *Gap-Time* goal is to travel the world, put that out to the universe in the form of a positive affirmation. It doesn't matter if you only have $2.00 in your bank account, or you don't even have a passport. Wake up every morning and send a positive thought out to the universe, "I am a world traveler." If your energy just confirms a past condition, then expect the condition to remain. But you can inwardly prepare for what you want rather than always affirming what has been. You can practice the life you want. Belief is powerful, and whatever we believe, we will subconsciously make manifest (Williamson, M., 2004). Remember—when you begin making positive changes through actions, such as practicing affirmations and sprinkling conversations with words like "synchronicity" and "serendipity," the people in your life may begin to ruffle their feathers. Don't allow them to rain on your parade. Maybe they're a crazymaker, or maybe they are a well-intentioned spouse who is reacting to a change in your behavior. Whatever the case, imagine them laughing when the unexpected shows up in your life. Hopefully, they will benefit from your positive powers.

We all have down times, and you may be thinking, "how in the earth do I do all this—think positively, open myself to possibilities, etc.—when I can barely get myself out of bed in the morning?" If that is the case, then just begin with baby steps—but begin. As you make small changes, you will begin to notice shifts in your feelings, thoughts, and energy. It won't happen overnight, but it will happen. An important thing to remember is that we all experience downtimes; it is how you choose to react and respond to them that will determine the outcome. It is important to remember that whatever place you're in, it is part of your journey—your own unique journey. You are supposed to be where you are right now.

If you're having a hard time motivating yourself, look to others for inspiration. I recently read an awesome book by a very gifted young writer, Elizabeth Gilbert, called *Eat, Pray, Love*. I'm sure you've likely heard of this bestseller, especially since Elizabeth appeared on Oprah. Elizabeth very eloquently and graciously shares her journey of self-discovery that begins at a time when Elizabeth is at a breaking point in her life. Her marriage is dissolving, her career success hasn't brought her the happiness she thought it would, and she is overwhelmed with confusion and anxiety. She embarks on a courageous journey through Italy, India and Indonesia, leaving behind everything she has ever known, and makes some discoveries she never dreamed possible. I encourage you to read it. I thoroughly enjoyed it because at its core is a story of strength, determination, faith, and starting over. Whether you're ending a marriage, a career, or grieving over a loss, life is about change and loss and recovery and discovery and growth and joy. And yes—there is joy. Always, there is joy.

In order to live positively in the present moment, what must you do? What fears must you let go of? What worries must you leave behind? What regrets must you relinquish? Let's start with a little exercise whereby you hand your worries over to God, a higher being, the Creator, or whatever it is you chose to name your higher power. If you want help paying the gas bill, so be it. If you want to hand over worries about a mysterious lump, a failing relationship, or a car in need of repair, write it down. If you need more pages, pull out your journal and keep going.

Dear (Fill in the Blank):
Today I am handing over my worries about:
_____
_____
_____
_____
_____
_____
_____
_____

No worry is too small or too large. If it keeps you up at night, write it down.

> Dear God:
>
> Today I am handing over my worries about:
> Tim's science project;
> My upcoming doctor's appointment;
> Dad's upcoming doctor's appointment;
> Paying off Jack's hospital bill;
> Flying to Anne Marie's wedding;
> Finding a dress to wear to Anne Marie's wedding.

Once your list is written, take a deep breath and know that your worries are no longer in your hands. Be open to the unexpected. Tune into the universe and don't be surprised if the miraculous happens. Recognize it when it does. In *Eat, Pray, Love*, Elizabeth writes a petition to God to help her with her divorce—not only are Elizabeth and her husband failing at their marriage, but they can't come to terms on the divorce. She mentally gets signatures from all the people in her life she thinks would sign the petition on her behalf—Mom, Dad, friends, co-workers, Bill and Hillary Clinton, Eleanor Roosevelt, Martin Scorcese, Bono, the Dalai Lama, Katharine Hepburn, St. Francis of Assisi. She goes on naming folks for about an hour until she feels a sense of security. Guess what happens next? I don't want to ruin the book for you, but shortly afterward her phone rings. It's her lawyer. "Great news . . . he just signed it [divorce papers]" (Gilbert, E., 2006).

As you release your worries and hand your problems over to God, higher power, Great Creator, etc., don't forget to ask for what you want—hopefully, you have a pretty clear vision by this point. It is your right to be happy and joyful. God wants you to live up to your highest potential, and I'm pretty sure He didn't say until he/she hits 65 years of age.

Now that you've handed over your worries, relax. "We think we have to lead, when all we really have to do is follow," says Marianne Williamson in *The Gift of Change*. There is a plan for our lives—God's plan—and it oversees exactly where we are and where we need to be going. As soon as we have learned to live most brightly in our present conditions, new and better ones will arrive immediately (Williamson, M., 2004).

Practice changing your circumstances by changing your thoughts. It is said that you will experience whatever comes to your mind after the words, "I am . . . ."

Get your pen out again and write as quickly as a thought comes into your head.

I am _____

I am _____

I am _____

I am _____

I am _____
I am _____
I am _____
I am _____
I am _____
I am _____

Your list can be anything you want it to be.
I am filled with joy.
I am financially secure.
I am going to Hawaii.
I am living abundantly.
I am physically fit.
I am a loving grandmother.
I am working at my dream job.
I am an engaging public speaker.
I am highly compensated for my skills.
I am in charge of my destiny.

    I have a confession to make. I didn't just come up with this magic formula. Millions of people have been doing this for thousands of years; perhaps you have been one of them. It's not rocket science, but sometimes we need gentle reminders. A little nudge or seeing it in black and white can be helpful if you're struggling with a thought or concept. I hope that this Chapter has helped prepare you for the unexpected gifts you are about to receive.

The world is its own magic.

Shunryu Suzuki (The Little Zen Companion)

Chapter 12

Putting it all together

"It's time to start living the life you've imagined."
—Henry James

Gap-Timers know that there is no set age at which one retires. You don't have to wait until you are 62, 65, or some other magical age to do what you really want to do. Retirement is not an exclusive economic event, nor is it a single lifestyle devoid of work and filled only with leisure activities (Anthony, M., 2001). *Gap-Timers* understand the treasure hunt of "self" and embracing their own *Gap-Time* Plan, which may include:

- Viewing their maturity as an asset rather than a frailty;
- Engaging in, instead of withdrawing from, their community, family, and friends;

- Seeking meaningful activities that take advantage of their creative talents rather than activities that merely fill time;
- Participating in community service, taking educational courses, and continuing to work, if that is one's desire.

Embrace your true self and whatever it is that you seek out to do or to be even if you decide to be a grouch (Sellers, 2006). Let your passions be your path. Give back to the community. Start a new career, lunch club, travel group, readers' circle, or [fill in the blank], or join one. Successful retirees don't change momentum; they change direction. "If I were to select the most important thing that will determine your retirement satisfaction, it would be the degree to which your expectations meet reality" (Schlossberg, N. K., 2004).

For every need fulfilled in our "work" life, we will need an equal or opposite need in the *Gap-Time*. Practice uncommon appreciation. Mother Teresa (winner of the Nobel Peace Prize) said, "There is more hunger for love and appreciation in this world than for bread." Jack Canfield describes three kinds of appreciation: auditory, visual, and kinesthetic (Canfield, J., 2005). "If you want to be a real pro at appreciation, you want to learn which kind of feedback makes the most impact on the person you are delivering it to" (Canfield, J., 2005). Take time to appreciate yourself, too. My good friend Nick always says, "one of the wonderful compensations in life is that no one can sincerely try to help another person without helping himself."

Start by listing all the advantages to entering the *Gap-Time*:

- More leisure time;
- Fewer family responsibilities (usually);
- Renewed sense of joy of learning;
- Freedom from schedules and routines;

- More friends your age with similar leisure time;
- A wider range of activities to keep you entertained, educated, and healthy; and
- An opportunity to be of service to your community (Weaver, 1997).

You probably thought of at least five or six more while reading this list.

Check to make sure you have the 12 qualities of happiness:

- Love;
- Optimism;
- Courage;
- A sense of freedom;
- Proactivity;
- Security;
- Health
- Spirituality;
- Altruism
- Perspective;
- Humor; and
- Purpose

(Baker & Stauth, 2003).

With these qualities, you will no longer need to search for happiness, it will find you.

It has been my privilege to know Ernest (Ernie) Banks, a great all-American (retired) baseball player and coach for the Chicago Cubs. One of Ernie's famous quotes is "You must try to generate happiness within yourself. If you aren't happy in one place, chances are you won't be happy anyplace." And so you should develop your *Gap-Time* plan to make you happy.

One part of Ernie's retirement is taking his slogans and quotes, as well as those of others, and having them embroidered on caps to sell or just give away. He asked me one day, "What's your slogan?" To which I replied, "I am NOT confused!" And now I have the cap to prove it! I am NOT confused and you need not be either. Confusion is similar to being in limbo, and that's not a good, productive place to be. Being in limbo can be stressful. The "not knowing" is where our stress comes from. Think about when you're waiting for medical test results—that waiting time is a pressure cooker. Once you know, however—even if the news isn't great—there is some relief. When there's confusion, it's because there is no clarity. Once you find clarity, you have a path and you can take action. You can always re-adjust and shift the plan, but go ahead and make a decision and run with it. Chances are that none of your decisions about your *Gap-Time* plans are going to be "life or death" decisions, so just flow with it. Have fun with it! Make a decision and move beyond the confusion and limbo.

You have the tools to map out your very own *Gap-Time* Plan. P-L-A-N to take action. Start with your skills and abilities and add your passion. Next, develop some *Gap-Time* objectives for the next two to three years. Do not compare your objectives with those of others. You are developing your *Gap-Time* plan to achieve your objectives and not for others. I placed as many resources at your fingertips in this book to make your *Gap-Time* journey focused and fun. Retirement coaches are available and can help you when you need a jumpstart or help getting "unstuck."

Art Linkletter gives us this poem to tie it all together:

"I never want to be what I want to be,
Because there's always something out there yet for me.
There's always one hill higher—with a better view,
Something waiting to be learned I never knew.
So until my days are over, never fully fill my cup.
Let me go on growing—up."

Art Linkletter

Gap-Time is your time on your terms. There's nothing in your way to stop you from enjoying sunny afternoons with friends, dancing when no one is looking, and laughing out loud. You have the freedom to travel the world and learn new cultures, ideas, and beliefs, or turn on the TV for a brief *Wheel of Fortune* indulgence. You design your own purpose. You select the people you like to be with, to learn from, and to connect with. Your senses allow you to enjoy love, to be loved, and to make a difference in the world. You pick a place that feels like home that provides the environment to create using your talents and energy.

"No trumpets sound when the important decisions of our life are made. Destiny is made known silently" (Agnes de Mille). Your *Gap-Time* warrants important decisions. Learn as much as you can. As my friend Dong says, "The more you know, the more you know." Ask and get answers. Research, analyze, and then act. "Bottom line is that when you are working, it is you who must make decisions and take action. The same is true about retirement. There is no one else but you who must act. You can't bury your head in the sand and let things happen," adds Dong.

Have a fabulous *Gap-Time* journey. "When you arrive at your destination(s)—and you will—make sure you have taken your heart with you" (Cohen, A. H., 2002). Wherever you go, you will find yourself. Set your goals and strive to achieve them. Remember that the process is as important as the product. The journey is as important as the destination. "A painting is never finished—it simply stops in interesting places" (Paul Gardner).

> The gaps are the thing. The gaps are the spirit's one home, the altitudes and latitudes so dazzlingly spare and clean that the spirit can discover itself like a once-blind man unbound. The gaps are the clefts in the rock where you cower to see the back parts of God; they are the fissures between mountains and cells the wind lances through, the icy narrowing fiords splitting the cliffs of mystery. Go up into the gaps. If you can find them, they shift and vanish too. Stalk the gaps. Squeak into a gap in the soil, turn and unlock—more than a maple—a universe.
>
> *Annie Dillard (The Little Zen Companion)*

References

Aizenman, N. C. & Constable P. (2007, September 14). "No lack of reasons, to keep on working." *The Washington Post*, pp. B1, B6.

Anthony, M. (2001). *The New Retire-Mentality*. Chicago, IL: Dearborn Trade Publishing.

Aratani, L. (2007, September 16). "Friendship Heights in Front Ranks of Senior Care." *The Washington Post*, p. A13.

Baker, D. & Stauth, C. (2003). *What Happy People Know*. New York, NY: St. Martin's Press.

Browne, J. (1998). *The Nine Fantasies that will Ruin your life (and the eight realities that will save you)*. New York, NY: Crown Publishers, Inc.

Cameron, J. (1992). *The Artist's Way A Spiritual Path to Higher Creativity*. New York, NY: G. P. Putnam's Son.

Canfield, J. (2005). *The Success Principles How to Get from Where You Are to Where You Want to Be*. New York, NY: HarperCollins Publishers, Inc.

Clinton, W. J. (2007). *Giving—How Each Of Us Can Change The World*. New York, NY: Knopf, Borzoi Books.

Cullinane, J & Fitzgerald, C. (2007). *The New Retirement The Ultimate Guide to The Rest of Your Life* (Rev. ed.). Rodale.

Cohen, A. H. (2002). *Why Your Life Sucks and What You Can Do About It.* San Diego, CA: Jodere Group.

Crandell, S. (2007). *Thinking About Tomorrow: Reinventing Yourself at Midlife.* New York, NY: Warner Wellness.

Crane, A. B. (June 26, 2007). Fame & Fortune: Entertainer Art Linkletter. Bankrate.com.

Donaho, M. W. & Meyer, J. L. (1976). *How To Get The Job You Want.* Englewood Cliffs, NJ: Prentice-Hall, Inc.

Dorsey, J. R. (2007). *My Reality Check Bounced!* New York, NY: Broadway Books.

Dreamer, O. M. (2005). *What we Ache For: Creativity and the Unfolding of Your Soul.* New York, NY: HarperCollins Publishers, Inc.

Dyer, W. W. (2006). *Inspiration Your Ultimate Calling.* Carlsbad, CA: Hay House, Inc.

Ehrmann, M. (1952). *Desiderata.*

Ettinger, W. H., Wright, B. S. & Blair, S. N. (2006). *Fitness After 50.* Champaign, IL: Human Kinetics.

Freudenheim, E. (2004). *Looking Forward: An Optimist's Guide to Retirement.* New York, NY: Stewart, Tabori & Chang.

Fulghum, R. (1986). *All I Really Need To Know I Learned In Kindergarten.* New York, NY: Ivy Books.

Gelb, M. J. (1998). *How to Think like Leonardo da Vinci: Seven Steps to Genius Every Day.* New York, NY: Dell Publishing.

Gilbert, E. (2006). *Eat, Pray, Love.* New York, NY: Penguin Group.

Gowen, A. (2007, September 16). Brave new boomers. *The Washington Post,* pp. A1, A12.

Griffith, S. (2005). *Work Your Way Around The World.* Oxford, England: Vacation Work Publications.

Hansen, M. V. & Linkletter, A. (2006). *How to Make the Rest of Your Life the Best of Your Life*. Nashville, TN: Thomas Nelson, Inc.

Harary, K. & Donahue, E. (1994). *Who Do You Think You Are?* New York, NY: HarperCollins Publishers, Inc.

Harkness, H. (1999). *Don't Stop the Career Clock*. Palo Alto, CA: Davies-Black Publishing.

Heidrich, R. E. (2005). *Senior Fitness*. New York, NY: Lantern Books.

Henderson, N. (2007, September 12). "Aging is inevitable, but boomers put 'old' on hold." *The Washington Post*, pp. H1, H5.

Hoff, B. (1982) *The Tao of Pooh*. New York, NY: Penguin Books.

Johnson, R. P. (2004). *What color is your retirement?* St. Louis, MO: Retirement Options.

Johnson, R. P. (2001). *The New Retirement* (1st ed.). St. Louis, MO: Retirement Options.

Kasich, J. (1998). *Courage Is Contagious*. New York, NY: Doubleday.

Keoghan, P. (2004). *No Opportunity Wasted (NOW)*. Emmaus, PA: Rodale.

Kerschner, H. K. & Hansan, J. E. (Eds.). (1996). *365 Ways . . . Retirees' Resource Guide for Productive Lifestyles*. Westport, CT: Greenwood Press.

Krannich, R. & Krannich, C. (2005). *I Want to Do Something Else, But I'm Not Sure What It Is*. Manassas Park, VA: IMPACT PUBLICATIONS.

Kustenmacher, T. (2004). *How to Simplify Your Life*. New York, NY: McGraw-Hill.

McGraw, P. C. (2001). *Self Matters: Creating Your Life from the Inside Out*. New York, NY: Simon & Schuster Source.

Marchione, M. (2007). *Survey: Seniors have sex into 70s and 80s*. [On-line]. Available: *http://www.boston.com/yourlife/health/women/articles/2007/08/22/survey_seniors_have_sex*.

Novelli, W. & Workman, B. (2006). *50+ Igniting a Revolution to Reinvent America*. New York, NY: St. Martin's Press.

Pink, D. (2005). *A Whole New Mind*.

Roizen, M. F. & Oz, M. C. (2006). *You, On A Diet: The Owner's Manual for Waist Management*. New York, NY: Free Press.

Rothman, R. (2006). *Early bird a memoir of premature retirement*. New York, NY: Simon & Schuster, Inc.

Schiller, David. (1994). *The Little Zen Companion*. New York, NY: Workman Publishing Company, Inc.

Schlossberg, N. K. (2004). *Retire Smart Retire Happy Finding Your True Path in Life*. Washington, DC: American Psychological Association.

Sellers, R. (Ed.). (2006). *Sixty Things To Do When You Turn Sixty*. Portland, ME: Ronnie Sellers Productions, Inc.

Sher, B. (1994). *I Could Do Anything If I Only Knew What It Was*. New York, NY: Delacorte Press.

Volz, J. (2000). *Sex After 60—Why Not?* [On-line]. Available: *http://www.webmd.com/sex-relationships/feasures/sex-seniors*.

Von Oech, R. (1998). *A Whack On The Side Of The Head*. New York, NY: Warner Books, Inc.

Wagner, T. & Day, B. (1998). *How To Enjoy Your Retirement*. Acton, MA: VanderWyk & Burnham.

Waxman, B. & Mendelson, R. A. (2006). *How to Love Your Retirement*. Atlanta, GA: Hundreds of Heads Books, LLC.

Weaver, F. (1997). *I'm Not As Old As I Used To Be*. New York, NY: Hyperion.

Weiss, R. S. (2005). *The Experience of Retirement*. Ithaca, NY: Cornell University Press. wikiHow (The How-to Manual That You Can Edit): *http://www.wikihow.com/Exercise-an-Open-Mind* (2007).

Williamson, M. (2004). *The Gift of Change: Spiritual Guidance for Living Your Best Life*. New York, NY: HarperCollins Publishers.

Martha's Bio

It is my pleasure to introduce you to the author. Martha Ann Madden, a native of Louisiana, has made significant impacts through her multi-faceted career that bridges education, executive management, government administration, the environment, and now, retirement. True to her own *Gap-Time* plan, Martha is using the talents she has acquired to change the course of retirement for many.

Martha is an accomplished achiever which is evidenced by the positions she has held and the successes that have followed her. Some of Martha's earlier achievements in boosting the numbers of appointments of women and minorities to boards and commissions in the state of Louisiana were captured in major national magazines, like *Working Women, Vogue,* and many others. When the 1984 World's Fair was held in New Orleans, Louisiana, Martha worked tirelessly to secure special international speakers for major events.

Ms. Madden has used her inheritance to fund scholarships at Louisiana State University, Centenary Colleges, and other colleges. Another project was to develop a collection of Louisiana's history, the Martha Madden Collection, at Northwestern State University. As the youngest Dean of Women in the South at Northeast Louisiana University and part of that time as the only woman dean at the university, Ms. Madden mentored, counseled, and advised thousands of students during her tenure. Madden sailed into the hearts and classrooms of numerous students as a regular Administrator on Semester at Sea—a shipboard classroom that goes around the world each semester.

As the secretary of the Department of Environmental Quality, Martha followed one of her passions—environmental work—and started another career. As the Louisiana Governor's point-of-contact for the state on all National Environmental Policy Act's reviews and approvals, Madden's attention turned to energy as a field of work. Later, Martha served on the Louisiana Governor's Energy Commission before working as the special assistant to the Office of Civilian Radioactive Waste Management at the U.S. Department of Energy in Washington, D.C.

Rounding out her federal government experience, Martha was appointed to serve on the Chemical Transportation Advisory Board with the U.S. Coast Guard appointed by the Secretary of the U.S. D.O.T. For 10 years, she was an appointed volunteer (Security Clearance) to the National Defense Executive Reservists (FEMA), Washington, D.C. Dedication and hard work took the form of volunteer appointments to two National Task Forces: (1) Chemical, Biological, Radiological and Nuclear Terrorism Task Force and (2) Cyber Threats of the Future Task Force. Ms. Madden excels in the worlds of academia and the environment. Madden has been given a vote of confidence among her colleagues and peers having been selected to the Board of Directors for the Women Council of Energy and the Environment.

Martha has traveled tirelessly to help those who had environmental concerns. Martha has creatively brought together people from widely different cultures to participate in environmental programs to design solutions to environmental problems.

Madden has a BS and MA from Southern Methodist University, Dallas, Texas and advanced graduate studies at Stanford University in California. She has traveled in 70 countries—over 5 million miles around the world—and lectured and/or attended United Nations Conferences, London Business School, and Taiwan University.

The recipient of countless awards and honors over the past 30 years, Ms. Madden received the 1987 State Conservation Award from the Louisiana Wildlife Federation for assisting in developing three volumes of an Environmental Educational Series, the U.S. EPA "Pioneer Award" for her work with the Small Business Assistance Program, Meritorious Service Recognition from the U. S. Department of Energy, the Outstanding Employee Award, Department of Energy, Office of Civilian Radioactive Waste, appointed to the Chemical Biological, Radiological and Nuclear Terrorism Task Force, and many other honors. In 2006, Martha was inducted into the Louisiana Women's Hall of Fame. At its 2007 Fall commencement, Northwestern State University (Louisiana) conferred upon Martha the Honorary Doctorate Degree of Humane Letters.

Memberships in national and state board commissions have included Save Our Coast Commission, Health and Environment Association of Louisiana, Louisiana Emergency Response Commission, and Louisiana Universities Marine Consortium.

Martha has expanded her career once again with another passion—retirement counseling. Helping individuals plan for success—with particular attention to adapting and enjoying the mature years through the discovery of new directions—keeps Martha vibrant.

If you are ready to explore new ways of living with more leisure time through inspiration, defining your life's meaning and purpose, don't wait another minute! Martha has something to tell you: "*Gap-Time.*"

~~~Annette H. Sharp